RATIC
MORALITY

RATIONAL MORALITY

a science of right and wrong

ROBERT JOHNSON

dangerous™
little books

First Published in Great Britain 2013
by Dangerous Little Books www.dangerouslittlebooks.com

© Robert Johnson

Cover image © www.istockphoto.com/mhj

*Dedicated to everyone who provided
insights in the development of this idea –
too many to name yet too important to forget.*

Contents

Introduction

Often there is confusion as to what morality means in the modern world — what relevance do ethics or morality have in our lives? The easiest way to explain is through the media portrayal of events that touch us all.

As I write this in the first months of 2013, there remain news reports and stories circulating in the UK media which relate to one of the most heavily covered stories of 2012. It began when interviews emerged in October 2012, airing on a TV documentary, alleging that the well-known celebrity Jimmy Savile (who died in 2011) had misused his position of power in order to commit sex crimes on five different females in the 1970's. As a result, the police began investigations and quickly gathered that he may have abused up to 25 victims. This figure rose dramatically over the coming months to around 450 potential victims coming forward (to date), with many of the targets of abuse being children or other vulnerable individuals.

A report released on January 11th 2013, jointly produced by the Met Police and the NSPCC, said the scale of the sexual abuse was 'unprecedented' and described Savile as a 'predatory sex offender'.[1] His victims ranged in age between 47 and just 8 years old–adding the further offence of paedophilic sex abuse to the already horrendous stories.

Unsurprisingly these crimes shocked and appalled the British public, as well as audiences around the world. We were shaken to our core to learn that a celebrity had managed to use his status to sexually abuse and exploit young children, patients dying in hospices and many other innocent victims. Many of the abused will be scarred for life, or may no longer be with us.

---

[1] http://www.nspcc.org.uk/news-and-views/our-news/child-protection-news/13-01-11-yewtree-report/yewtree-report-pdf_wdf93652.pdf

It is our reaction to these crimes that underpin our *ethics*. We don't just find Savile's actions distasteful, we find them *morally* abhorrent. We don't think it is okay to do what he did and we think he should have been stopped from doing so. This is *morality*, and that we desperately desire for sex offenders like Savile to be stopped, or locked up, shows our will for there to be an observed *moral code*. We don't think that someone like Savile should be allowed to do what he likes at the victims' expense, so we don't believe that morality should be *relative* to each person and instead we think that it should be *objectively* applied to anyone who does what he did (regardless of their position of power and influence or personal tastes).

Already it has been easy to explain the idea of morality and ethics at an important level. By using the examples of news stories it is easy to show what ethics are, how strongly we want them and that we want this system of morality to be objectively applied. This, in a nutshell, is how ethics work.

This might lead you to ask, what is the purpose of this book, if we already have an observed and demonstrable form of morality in society? Well, another major news story doing the rounds might explain it: same sex marriage. For the past few years same sex marriage has been debated, and was opposed by many Republicans (among others) in the US and many Conservatives in the UK. Still many states in the US do not allow for gay marriage, and the UK plans to allow for it although does not compel any religious group to perform same sex marriage services. Unlike in cases of sex abuse, opinion is not as unified on the moral issue of gay marriage. There are passionate voices arguing for it and against it.

Yet, if one is to analyse the content of the arguments on same sex marriage, there really isn't a big debate to be had. Religious groups have no evidence for their own spiritual beliefs (being, as they are, personally posited truths), and yet the marriage ceremonies which they can perform have legal recognition (and legal benefits, in some places). However, they are being legally allowed to discriminate based on sexual orientation when it comes to performing these ceremonies, even though the law says that discrimination is illegal as a general matter.

There are only two possible, rational solutions to the same-sex marriage issue when we are given these facts as outlined above. The first is that religious groups are forced to allow same sex couples to marry, so as not to legally discriminate based on their own personal opinions. The second is that religious groups give up the legal and state-influencing powers they have, due to the spiritual, illegal and non-rational justification they wish to give to discrimination. These are the only two moral options: there is no middle ground, just as there isn't with the Savile case. Doing anything other than this (such as allowing same sex marriage, but not making all institutions that need to recognise it do so; as has happened in the UK) is to arbitrarily allow for discrimination. That is an abuse of the kind of fairness which we seem to want in cases like Savile's.

What the same sex marriage debate shows is that although we have a functioning system of morality in some areas (such as where societal opinion is rationally unified against sex abuse), it is completely uninformed in others (where it should be converged against discrimination in the case of gay marriage, for example).

The analysis of these two news stories gives a good grounding on what morality is, but also with the problem of morality in society. Almost everyone recognises the immorality of what Savile did, probably because it is already legally and culturally forbidden, and yet relatively few recognise or are disgusted by the immorality of discrimination or other rationally indefensible moral acts that are not already culturally forbidden. We seem to understand the reason that we need morality, as exemplified by our opinions on things like murder and violent abuse, but we seem to misunderstand that morality doesn't just stop with what we currently find as immoral; it extends to things we may never even have thought about before, or things that we don't currently legislate for. It should work based on fairness, not familiarity.

These stories show that ethics is still an extremely relevant subject. We want the vulnerable to be protected, we want aggressors to be stopped and we want fairness to persevere. We may wish to sum up the theoretical issues that these very different examples raise in three sets of questions:

1. Should morality be relative, or objective?

Is it definitely our split personal opinions on gay marriage that are wrong, or are we instead wrong to have a largely unified opinion against sex crime? Can an objective view of morality even be defensible within a modern, scientific view of the world, when morality seems to be opinion based and not fact based? In other words, how can an opinion on a moral issue be equated with being a moral fact, in the same way that physical science like physics or chemistry talks about facts? Are we deluding ourselves?

2. If morality is objective, then how can we fully judge what is right and what is wrong?

How do we know what is objectively wrong and what is objectively permissible, and how do we best make these decisions?

3. What is the real world effect for each of us once we have these answers?

What would a rational morality have us do? And why should we care to do it?

Don't worry if these questions feel very vague or unexplained for now, as they will be explained in detail at different stages. Roughly speaking, the following pages are my attempt to answer these questions — and a few more — whilst formulating a fresh, modern and more rational way to think about morality. A way in which morality can be viewed as a form of science. If at any stage things seem like they have gotten too complex, or too theoretical, always draw it back to these kinds of simple questions; ethics is about events and happenings in the real world, and should be able to be understood by anyone. The theory, as referenced throughout, only exists so as to back up or else correct our opinions, by pointing out a more thorough understanding of the real world. That's all theory is and thus it should never be needlessly complex. This is my adopted philosophy, and there's no better place to quote one of my favourite historical influences, William of Ockham:

"It is pointless to do with more what can be done with fewer."

I hope that the influence of this single line will become obvious the more you read.

Rob Johnson, March 2013

Rational morality: a brief synopsis

To give you an idea of the structure of the book, the first half of rational morality (chapters 1-4) deal with the theory: does there currently exist a scientific theory of morality, what would one look like, why do we need it, etc. It develops what a rational form of morality would look like and how such a theory would deal with classic philosophical issues such as the is-ought problem (whilst explaining why those problems matter in a simple manner). The first half also approaches some criticisms of the ideas necessary in a rational theory of morality, as well as a few other brief digressions in order to explore the issue more thoroughly. I would suggest that these four chapters are read chronologically, as they explain the problems with moral philosophy, solve them and then defend my solution (in that order).

The second half of the book (5-10) engages practical ethics, examples of rational morality in action and a brief introduction of a number of areas within the burgeoning subject of moral science. These kinds of ideas form the backbone of what rational morality would look like in the real world, to sit alongside the largely theoretical formulation of ideas in the first half. From atheism to animal ethics to determinism, I hope this part will provoke great debate as well as form the foundation for the incorporation of current evidence and reason into moral science.

1. *Marrying Morality with Reality*

HOW DO WE DECIDE WHAT'S RIGHT AND WRONG?

On 13th February 2012, a prominent politician (one of the most influential decision makers in Britain[2]) published a much referenced article in a British newspaper entitled 'We stand side by side with the Pope in fighting for faith'[3]. In it, Baroness Warsi (the minister in question) notes that Europe needs to be "more confident and more comfortable in its Christianity" and warns against "militant secularisation" which "demonstrates similar traits to totalitarian regimes".

One might be puzzled by such statements; after all Britain doesn't seem overly "militant" in its secularism[4]. I don't see anyone burning down churches or mosques in the name of atheism, for example, and those who most militantly advocate secularism seem to do so with no more aggression than to speak or write about it. Quite a long way from totalitarian regimes, one might argue. People have naturally waned from Christianity over the years, undoubtedly, but militant secularism seems like an overstatement. This natural move toward secularisation is even understandable. There's no evidence for untestable assertions like that of 'God', and people seem to have naturally recognised that religion might just be wishful thinking. The late Christopher Hitchens perhaps summarised it best when he wrote that "I was educated by Sir Karl Popper to

---

[2] At the time, the politician in question was both a cabinet minister – which is one of the primary people consulted on government decisions and policy – and co-chairman of the ruling party.

[3] http://www.telegraph.co.uk/news/religion/9080441/We-stand-side-by-side-with-the-Pope-in-fighting-for-faith.html

[4] Then Prime Minister, David Cameron, himself issued pro-religious sentiments in 2011, claiming that the UK is a Christian country and "should not be afraid to say so" (http://www.bbc.co.uk/news/uk-politics-16224394). If nothing else, this shows that Britain is far from militant in its secularism – the head of state himself pushes the idea of the state as religious, not secular.

believe that a theory that is unfalsifiable is to that extent a weak one." [5] As was I.

Warsi's entire article seems a bit odd, that is until you read her justification for making such statements: "to create a more just society, people need to feel stronger in their religious identities and more confident in their creeds"

Unwittingly, in an impassioned defence of religion, Warsi places her finger right on the pulse of what is arguably the biggest innate problem we face as a society and a species. With the ever increasing secularisation of society, stemming from an entirely reasonable rejection of religion, there also seems to be an air of moral vacancy. It pours from the gap left by our previous 'moral rule bearer' of religion and seems to ask us to conclude that without God to set the rules, morality must be flexible and relative else non-existent.[6]

As such, society is facing a crisis of confusion when it comes to moral inclinations. On the one hand, we want to oppose murder, rape and hundreds of other heinous acts of cruelty which are currently against the law, in the most fundamental manner. The media and our personal opinions are still outraged by these kinds of acts against innocent victims. On the other hand, we seem to be in a position of

---

[5] Quoted in *God is Not Great*. Hitchens is referring to the work of the great philosopher of science, Karl Popper, whose work is still a guiding influence in defending and promoting the reasons why science is such a wonderful method of truth finding.
[6] One study that show this in particular, http://onthehuman.org/2010/12/objective-moral-truths/. Knobe notes that there is no evidence to show that people believe morality to be objective, and explains various studies on the subject which show that several types of people tend toward moral relativism. Most interestingly, when discussing Feltz and Cokely: "they conducted a study in which they measured both openness to experience and belief in moral relativism...The higher a participant was in openness to experience, the more likely that participant was to give a relativist answer." Knobe discusses similar findings from Goodwin and Darley which showed that people who consider a variety of possibilities in answering questions are also more inclined to offer relativist answers. These two studies heavily support the idea that people who are more open to experience, or more open to other views, show an inclination to moral relativism. This backs up common sense, as our moral rules are built upon Abrahamic religious foundations, so when people begin shedding this as the sole acceptable viewpoint, they tend toward a more accepting view of other types. Hence they tend toward moral relativism. This backs up my point that as society becomes more secular, rightly or wrongly it tends toward moral relativism.

understanding that morality is largely relative and thus any newly thought moral or immoral acts we see people engaging in (ethical veganism as moral, or deforestation as immoral, for example) are a matter of subjective 'choice' rather than in any sense right or wrong[7]. We tend to take the position that what is illegal is wrong, but that so long as something is legal it is acceptable and thereby only to be taken as immoral in relation to personal tastes. Law reflects objective wrongs, whilst all others are subjective.

This creates a paradoxical tension, as law itself is primarily a reflection of our majority societal opinions. So if we want to oppose something that's against the law then we need to be able justify why we oppose it — we *make law, it doesn't make us* — and similarly we need to leave the law open for new things which we discover to be immoral, in order to legally forbid them. But how can we do this if we want to claim that doing right or wrong is 'just a choice'? How can we believe that morality is both objective and subjective: that some things are wrong, yet others of the same ferocity are a matter of choice? To understand the issue more completely, we need to explore the topics involved.

LAW AS A REFLECTION OF SOCIAL OPINION

There is no 'all seeing eye' who creates and maintains the juridical system. In modern democratic systems laws are invented and indeed amended by us. This simple observation quashes the idea that something being against the law makes it immoral, or that something being perfectly legal makes it acceptable. As history progresses laws will change and they thus reflect societal opinion of the time, rather than the ultimate answer on whether an act is morally right or wrong.

---

[7] Of course, one would have to agree veganism was a coherent, rational moral choice in the first place – a claim doubted by both some of those in favour of animal rights and those against it. And also that deforestation is immoral. However here I use them as examples, as people often put these down to a notion of "each to their own" rather than a matter of right and wrong. We don't do this with things like murder, or rape, so it is interesting that we feel the need to do it with moral issues that are not illegal.

The most popular examples to demonstrate this point often focus on human slavery, or other things we now find morally abhorrent but which a few hundred years ago may have been perfectly legal. In fact one may not be far wrong in claiming everything we now view as immoral would have been legal somewhere, at some point in history (take race-based slavery, or the ownership of women as examples). And unsurprisingly, many things we now find acceptable or even moral (such as challenging scientific conclusions with new evidence or criticising religious doctrine by pointing to its inherent paradoxes or lack of evidence) would have been deemed morally unacceptable in some society at some point. Law is merely the reflection of the current societal attitudes and cannot be used as justification for moral stances any more than we can justify them with the idea that we *can* physically commit said acts. This statement is summed up nicely by the phrase '*The way things are does not justify the way they ought to be*'. I *could* jump out of my second floor window right now and likely break a bone or two, but this does not imply I *should*. The laws of physics and the laws of the land share in *allowing* us to commit ourselves to certain actions, but neither could be taken as sole *moral justification* for doing so.

The most likely explanation for the widespread belief in current moral norms, and the corresponding offering of moral guidance solely to law, was uncovered by Eidelman et al in a study called The Existence Bias.[8] The authors demonstrated that "people treat the mere existence of something as evidence of its goodness...the status quo is seen as good, right...and desirable." Studies such as this can explain why our problematic and irrational beliefs formed, but if the status quo does not conclusively tell us what is acceptable and what is wrong, then what does? The natural act is to begin applying scepticism to the subject of morality.

---

[8] The Existence Bias. Journal of Personality and Social Psychology 2009, Vol. 97, No. 5, 765-775. Eidelman, S., Pattershall, J. and Crandall, C.S.

DOES MORALITY EVEN EXIST?

Religious justification

The oldest and arguably still the most popular reason for invoking a notion of morality is down to religion. If God exists and has rules he wants us to follow, then these are moral facts. We can thus judge the wrongness or acceptability of any action with reference to whether God approves or not.

Society increasingly rejects this form of moral theory though, with Western society (and indeed states within Africa and Asia) now providing examples of almost entirely secular governments[9]. There is no way to be kind in debunking this religious justification for morality logically, at least not without offending someone. However, we live in a world where science moves us forward and is valued based on the fact that it needs to *demonstrate* (or at least conclusively and rationally imply) that which it wants to confirm as true, rather than merely announcing it. So when such an excellent and developed system for finding truth exists, why on earth is anyone using the justification of something which we have no evidence for at all? One by one we have discarded beliefs formed out of myth and tradition. The most notable remaining myth in society is religion and its God(s). No longer can this continue, without evidence or rational implication, to be considered useful in academic or rational discussion.

There is no relevance in the 21st century to an argument that says *'A force/man which I have no evidence for, and which I believe in simply because of my own personal valuing of a naively*

---

[9] We hear many examples of this: Sweden, Netherlands and an increasing number of non-European countries around the world claim to be secular (it is difficult to measure just how many states are truly secular in approach). The most interesting case of secularisation in government is in Honduras, where the following guarantee of religious separation from government can be found in Article 77 of the constitution (translated): "It guarantees the free exercise of all religions and cults without precedence, provided they do not contravene the laws and public order. The ministers of different religions, may not hold public office or engage in any form of political propaganda, on grounds of religion or using as a means to that end of the religious beliefs of the people." One wonders how different political campaigns in hugely influential countries like the US would look with this kind of approach.

trusting mental occurrence called faith, should tell me what to do. My proof is that it is written in a book/I simply say it is true'. We can respect religious people as much as we want within society, but if we take issues like morality seriously we should not be subjecting it to ideas for which there is no evidence. God may be a more serious concept for people than the flying spaghetti monster[10], but when we are discussing rationally they should share equal, non-existent pull. Similarly opinions about 'forces' or 'energies' which do not resemble classic ideas of God, but which claim to provide moral ideas (like Karma, for instance) should be tested and subjected to the rigours of reason. A scientist would be rightly ignored, and perhaps even laughed out of conferences for stating that gravity is not a justifiable force, but that we're attracted to the ground because strong, invisible, prehistoric jelly covers the Earth's surface. And yet religious and spiritual ideas, like the existence of God, or Karma, hold the same level of evidence. Advancement is about proving past ideas wrong, or discarding them based on what we now know in order to develop our knowledge base. But if we can't discard something there's zero evidence for, then there's little point in trying to discard anything and the whole system suffers a major flaw.

It is true that not every piece of scientific knowledge we have can be conclusively supported, indeed theoretical science deals with ideas which we may as yet have no evidence to test with. However each and every one of these 'theories' are required because we know there must be *a* theory. Take quantum mechanics, where several theories battle for describing several different concepts which as yet we have been unable to conclusively test. Even if we were never able to test them, we still know that there must be *a* theory that is correct, as we see activity that must work based on some law. Thus there is need to devise a theory that explains it. However, ideas like religion are not theories in the same manner. We have no need to imply that a theory of religion is needed, as

10 http://www.venganza.org/

the universe looks precisely as it should look were there to be no God, and were we to be individuals without a perfect ability to understand how the universe works. If we could say the same about physics at the quantum level-that it looks precisely how it should look if there were no quantum theories-then quantum theory would be a mute subject which would not be considered science. We see subatomic particles appear to behave in ways we need explanation for though and so we create theories of explanation to test. We have never come across an event with which we need to create a theory of God to explain and furthermore, what kind of idea could have us so perplexed that culturally invented icons and mythologies are a good explanation? It is best to remember that God was created in human minds, there is no evidence for him, and that we've no need to invoke a theory of God in order to explain anything. If you have to use God as an explanation for something then all kinds of other ideas are back on the table also: Thor, Allah, Superman, The Flying Spaghetti Monster, Spiderman, an omnipotent Barbie or an all seeing alien cockroach are just a tiny fraction of an infinite number of explanations that work as well as a theory of God. It is only when you consider the sheer number of other made up theories which work just as well as God in the situations where God could possibly be required as an explanation, that you realise just how poor an explanation it is. If there is something we can't explain then a cultural myth is not likely to be the answer we are searching for. 'Randomness' or 'chance' is actually always going to be a better explanation than 'God', as it is always more likely that things happen entirely naturally but in a way we can't fathom and so have to put down as 'chance', than it is that they happen because an omnipotent immaterial being created them.

As a result of ideas like this, and given the ever increasing secularisation of society over the years, we've begun to grow away from these irrational religious ideals of morality as a factual, God given concept. Previously, many societies were largely ruled by the idea that a God or benevolent force had set the rules and we must follow them, else we might be punished in some way[11]. Many Western court rooms, which dealt with such laws here on Earth, started proceedings with oaths on the bible[12]. However, as science has gotten more capable, so has our ability to doubt the existence of a Creator or Lord of any kind; and with it the ability to regard the leftovers from these more religious times with suspicion.

The rational debunking of this first aspect, religion, has left morality in the firing line. Religion is the easiest way to justify morality, as it requires no evidence. So if there is no God setting moral rules, how do such rules realistically exist in the first place? After all, scientists are hardly climbing mountains to uncover new moral facts underneath rocks, or implying the existence of moral facts in reactions after the collision of particles at a sub-atomic level. If God isn't setting objective moral laws, how do they exist?

The spiritual get out clause'?

It's true that many admit the fallibility of religious conceptions of morality in modern society, however a good chunk of those people believe there is an irrational 'get out clause' in science, which means spiritual arguments are valid, and thereby we can base our morality around what would have been irrational ideas like 'independent moral facts'[13]. With a regular reference to quantum mechanics (an area of science that proves very popular in religious and spiritual discussions due to it being fundamentally misunderstood by many people), the argument goes that some areas of science conclusively prove that the laws of physics are paradoxical.

---

[11] Believed punishments would vary depending on the society – examples include Karmic rebuttals within your own life, or an after-life justice like heaven and hell depending on the society.

[12] A practice continued to this day in countries like the USA.

[13] An 'independent moral fact' is my way of referencing the idea that a moral fact exists in exactly the same way a physics or biology fact does – people who believe in 'independent moral facts' (primarily known as 'moral realists') believe that these facts exists out-with human society, and are facts that we are simply uncovering. They believe that our intuitions or calculations or logic can uncover these pre-existing facts, in the same way that we can uncover facts in science through investigation.

Hence we do not know science to be a reliable, flawless method, and spiritual ideas are perfectly valid.

Indeed quantum mechanics is an interesting modern form of scientific investigation, which baffled (and still baffles) many physicists. Danish physicist Niels Bohr famously said "Anyone who is not shocked by quantum theory has not understood it." Whilst the infamous Richard Feynman is thought to have elaborated further with "If you think you understand quantum mechanics, you don't understand quantum mechanics."[14] It's little wonder that people have leapt on the subject in order to provide evidence for the mysterious. It's not at all difficult to find spiritual groups and influenced companies who mangle the ideas or terminology of quantum mechanics in order to make a profit or create a justification for nonsense.[15]

It truly is a fascinating discipline, and not just because of its counter-intuitive results. The entire area demonstrates the real strengths of science: that whatever ideas are held to be correct should be constantly challenged if new evidence is uncovered. Science does not stick to rigid accounts of events which do not hold to be true, and instead develops as our understanding of the world develops. Quantum mechanics would not be studied under the umbrella of science at all if scientists were not held strictly to these high standards.

But what is either a dishonest claim or a simple misunderstanding is the idea that areas like quantum mechanics mean spiritual 'theories' should be supported. Sure, science is a

---

[14] Bohr As quoted in *Meeting the Universe Halfway* (2007) by Karen Michelle Barad, p. 254, with a footnote citing *The Philosophical Writings of Niels Bohr* (1998). No-one can be certain that Feynman stated his attributed quote, although many people attest that it was definitely his style! In any case, the quote is an interesting one.

[15] Primarily those making profit tend to exploit the 'quantum healing' phenomenon, for which even the community run Wikipedia defines as a "pseudo-scientific mixture of ideas drawing on quantum mechanics…"
(http://en.wikipedia.org/wiki/Quantum_healing)
Those working in ethics use and abuse quantum mechanics in all kind of ways, and in debates I have variously encountered it as being used in a circular attempt to disprove determinism (and hence show that any rational argument against independent moral facts is flawed by virtue of relying on rationality as a marker of truth).

developing system which constantly evolves and so can often hold truths which it later proves to be wrong. But the truths it holds are not personally posited, nor the subject of desires, individual experiences or armchair philosophical inquiry. Every truth held in science (however wrong it may prove to be in the future) is held precisely because it makes sense with what we know of the world, and is the best account we have in relation to the evidence. A spiritual idea that says we can't prove everything with science, or that science is wrong by virtue of its evolution, is engaging in methodological hyperbole or else is simply misguided. Science is built to take into account the changing nature of truth based on increasing levels of evidence, so it is telling that it has yet to embrace the supernatural as having positive truth values.

Another idea the spiritualist will often point to is the 'big bang' and the question of "what came before it?" The answer science predicts of nothingness is not a shot in the dark so much as the best supported answer we have. There is no evidence that there was anything before the big bang, but there is evidence to suggest there was a big bang. The spiritualist who claims nothingness cannot create something (however intuitive this is) can't then posit a spiritual idea, which there is no evidence for, as true due to this paradox which they have identified. The fact is that there is less evidence for any spiritual idea you can think of (whether it be of a supernatural force, or energy…the positions appear to be limitless) than there is for nothingness. The beauty of admitting there may have been nothing, but that science hasn't yet developed to a space where we can begin to answer these questions fully yet (possibly because the problem is our limits of understanding 'space-time', rather than that the answer is paradoxical), is in the fact that we are being honest. The dishonesty of claiming it was a God, or a similarly irrational spiritual idea is clear to see. And as the now infamous example of the flying spaghetti monster shows, it makes no sense to posit these equally unsupported spiritual ideas which claim to answer questions they couldn't possibly know the solution to. These responses are the equivalent of making answers up. If you can't figure out the answer to a mathematical problem, you don't just make an answer up. This might be a good bet if you want to maximise your chances on an exam, but a developing body of knowledge cannot work when it's filled with random guesses.

The mathematics comparison

A popular, more rational (though still arguably spiritual) argument for asserting independent moral facts (moral facts which are there for us to investigate and uncover, and not created by humans or society) comes from comparing morality with other 'non-physical' concepts that we do think exist, like mathematics. If it is true that Pi = 3.14159265... (and so on), despite Pi not being a physical fact found under rocks or on mountains either, then why can't it be true that murder is wrong? Both appear to be non-physical facts so why can't both have independent truth values? This, in a nutshell, is the argument that our intuitions about morality relate to moral facts, in the same way that our intuitions about mathematics relate to mathematical facts. This is clearly a step up in logic from the basic religious and spiritual argument.

The comparison, though compelling at first glance, is still illegitimate though. Rational concepts, like mathematics, which are not rooted directly in physical facts about the world stem from our understanding and investigated evidence in it. For example, the sum '2+2=4' is essentially linguistic symbolism for seeing two things, and adding that same amount of things again, so as we can symbolise the resulting amount (4) in our communication rather than having to be experiencing it at the time. No matter how complex and abstract mathematics can get, and no matter how removed from the world it can seem, you can always reduce any mathematical problem back to these initial observations if you really put in the effort. There is real world relation that supports the notion of 2+2=4, and the symbolic substitution of language is referencing it, not referencing some intuitive and non-physical concept. Maths is a symbolic way to explain real world events, in ever increasing complexity, for the furtherance of human understanding without the inconvenience of having to get a million things, and add a million things to it, to show the resulting two million. This is an explanation of the mathematical concept of *addition* but it also works for every form of maths when it is related back. Maths is a short hand for real objects and measurements.

What about the more theoretical numbers, like Pi, which don't obviously relate to real world objects? Well, they are still remarkably easy to draw back to real world evidence. For example, Pi is infinite in digits, and we'll likely never know every last digit which it constitutes[16]. However this does not mean our belief in Pi is abstract like our belief in moral facts would be. Pi represents a very real concept, and we know it must exist from observations about Euclidean circles and the relation of their circumference to their diameter. It is a fact that Pi, as a concept, exists and if you reduce it back to where it is being implied into existence, then you come back to those millions of measurements of circles made during the history of human civilisation. These measurements themselves are made with rulers, measured out and marked by numbers in a certain order; the order of the numbers being those same things which are symbolically referencing real world objects (which we know exist from observing 2 stones + 2 stones, and referring to those 2 sets of 2 as 4, which in turn tells us the order of 1, 2, 3, 4, etc.). Like words creating sentences, we create mathematical arguments with symbols, but they reference real, physical facts if reduced back–like with any words. And hence the meaning of words and numbers are highly factual and based in the materialist, scientific world.

So, mathematics does not exist out-with the physical world; it is, however indirectly, implied from observations at

---

[16] We can't know every number of Pi without significant answers as to the problems with paradoxes, anyway – infinity has to end somewhere doesn't it?! Well no, but there's no saying that rational inquiry cannot solve the problems with paradoxes which are currently posed and provide some finite figure for Pi, theoretically.

every point. But how can the same thing be said of morality? Morality is about intuitions — intuitions implanted in us by a rich evolutionary history. It didn't evolve when the concept of God was invented and this is proved (or as 'proved' as we can hope human knowledge to attain) by the fact that we see some altruistic behaviour in other species[17], and also by the existence of mirror neurons, which will be explained later on. And furthermore, given that everything we do is possible because of evolutionary development (morality is no different), then what makes moral facts a true concept, but not religious facts? Or colour facts? One could imply the factuality of any concept by reference to the fact we have intuitions about it, and if one doesn't agree that there is a universal, independent fact of what is the 'best colour' then that casts serious doubt on the consistency of arguing that there are acts which violate universal facts about morality. People's intuitions disagree on things as extremely immoral as murder, and hence we see people committing murder. So to pretend that intuitions tell us 'murder is wrong' is simply to push your own intuitions as correct rather than the murderer's, on the arbitrary basis that he isn't you, or perhaps that he isn't in agreement with the majority of you. If you disagree with him about mathematics, one of you can most likely be proved right with linguistic argumentation which draws back to real world truths, whereas the same cannot be said about disagreements on morality, in which we can only ever push our own opinions.

So although mathematics might involve intuitions at some point (there might be an intuition to measure things, or a seemingly innate intuition that 4 is bigger than 3), they are of a very different type to morality. We can prove or disprove our mathematical inclinations by reference to facts in the world, and when they are so abstract as to defy current methods of proof (or even defy all methods of proof

---

[17] Proof which should be fairly strongly referenced, unless one wants to argue that other animals inherently believe in God and act morally as a result of this. A hypothesis one would struggle to find any support for.

forevermore) we can at least go back and provide reasons why we think it is the case (reducing back to physical facts and noting the reasons why there must be a mathematical law which the numbers are adhering to). Indeed if a theory doesn't match up with the facts we can prove about mathematics, then we can discard it and remain in search of a better answer which might be the true fact on the issue. We can even be unsure if it is truly knowable.

But what happens if we hold morality to these same rigours that other non-physical facts (like mathematical facts) have to be held to? We can't even get started, as morality isn't derived from evidence and facts like mathematics is. We can say someone is being murdered (a fact), and that we feel bad about it (a fact), but how can we say that it is right to feel bad about it because there is a universal fact that 'murder is wrong', which this emotion is referring to? Such a physical fact doesn't, and can't, exist. Moreover if classic morality passes this test of reason by virtue of it relating to intuition, then so can any belief. Realistically speaking, the fact I feel things doesn't make it true that the feeling is correct, and similarly the fact I want something to be wrong doesn't make it wrong. This is the argument that flaws religious thought as a rational matter, and it also does away with the idea that there are independent moral facts that we can search for.

It seems fair to say the mathematics comparison is simply inaccurate, and if moral facts do exist they certainly aren't of the type that says intuition is referring to independent moral facts about the universe. We need a more relativist form of morality in order to marry it with reality, one which takes into account the fact that morality exists because evolution has developed it into us as a social tool, and which does not make claims about there being non-physical facts floating in the universe to which our intuitions can be right or wrong in relation to.

THE EVOLUTION OF MORALITY

As touched upon in the last paragraph, morality is a socially evolved trait. In Dawkins update on Darwin's theory of evolution[18], he notes that our bodies are vehicles for genes which although selfish in wanting to reproduce (and hence have spawned complex structures of tissue and forms of intelligence over the millions of years that they have been evolving, in order to protect and enhance their ability to play the reproduction game), they have not evolved into structures that are selfish in the classic 'survival of the fittest' type, as many people erroneously think. Whilst selfishness may be a useful trait, so is altruism and the ability to cooperate, among others. The 'fittest' refers to those who utilise the best traits, in the most successful way, not some tooth and claw idealism (although it might manifest this way in many species).

As a result, and as societies of these individuals (made up of selfish genes) have grown more complex, we see that all types of persons can thrive in society. But moreover, in a social society fully selfish individuals will not always be reproductively successful. Reproduction is about carrying genes on, and our natural desire to protect our own genes is in competition with our natural desires to protect our children and parents (who share on average 50% of our genes), our brothers and sisters (who also share around 50%), and perhaps more relevantly we have developed–at times long before we could be called humans–a social desire to protect others as a mutual matter of developing both a society and fulfilling social relationships in which ourselves, our young and our relatives are looked after with minimised risk of them being destroyed.

Dawkins himself is not at pains to explain selfish or sociopathic behaviour which society still suffers. It becomes apparent that in any society where people are kind to one another outside of family bonds, this will leave opportunity for a few 'users' to take advantage of kindness and to flourish

---

[18] *The Selfish Gene*, Richard Dawkins

without returning any kindness back into society. But in several species, we see 'users' to be rare. Dawkins highlights the examples of vampire bats, from the work of G.S Wilkinson[19], to show why this might be. Vampire bats feed at night and they don't often get lucky with it, but when they do hit a feed they tend to get a big one. As a result, Wilkinson saw many cases of altruism whereby bats would feed others who hadn't gotten a feed from the night (the majority were kin: at least 77 out of 110 cases). This is a pay-off that appears to occur in nature in several species, and is an evolutionarily successful one. And when tested under controlled conditions, the bats themselves would withhold feed from starving bats in other groups who were not known to be 'givers' previously. In other words, if there is a risk you are a 'user', you are much less likely to get help in your hour of need. Hence 'users' do not do well.

In a society as developed as human civilisation, with social stigma and legal punishments resulting in 'users' getting a reputation and most likely comeuppance (a system well beyond the complexity of any bat societies), it isn't a great strategy to be selfish in all of your dealings with others. Similarly, one might claim that the biggest benefit to us all is a rational understanding of altruism as a universal concept (this is something I will discuss throughout by discussing the rationality of morality as a purely selfish matter, though it is certainly not what I am advocating). If it makes evolutionary sense for many other species to develop altruistic tendencies in more basic social scenarios, we can multiply this need a great deal to recognise how important it is in consciously monitored, complex civilisations like that of human beings. We can also show that given our rational abilities, we can consciously understand the need not to be users and form effective flourishing for everyone to a much better degree. At least in theory.

---

[19] *The Selfish Gene,* p 231. Original source is Wilkinson, G. S. (1984) Reciprocal food-sharing in the vampire bat. *Nature* **308**, 181-4.

As Dawkins brings this research together, one thing becomes obvious. Morality is not a trait that evolved solely in human beings. Altruism is a trait present in a variety of other species, and this shows it plays a vital role in the game of gene reproduction. Morality at its most basic point is a development of wanting to protect our genes, like the more basic kind of morality in the vampire bats, rather than referring to a development of 'intuitions' with which to identify separate, independent moral facts existing in the universe. This is not to say certain objective moral facts cannot exist (as I will examine later), but independent moral facts like this certainly are the stuff of fantasy, as is the idea that selfishness is some desirable, natural characteristic that it is 'rational' and optimal to explicitly hold and act upon.

RELATIVE AND OBJECTIVE ETHICS

This basic understanding of how morality evolved, and why, is vital to forming a moral theory. The theory that initially seems to be best placed in taking it on board is moral relativism. The most rational current form of which is the idea that morality as we conceive it doesn't exist, is a social construct, and thus should be deemed relative. There are no independent moral facts hiding under rocks or in trees, and our intuitions about morality are simply tools for social success, instilled in us by millions of years of evolution. So there should be no need to hold people to moral laws that do not really exist. It often manifests as cultural relativism, which notes that if a code of morality exists in any culture we should respect that as having its own truth values within that culture. Morality in any given culture is a socially useful tool and we should just follow moral laws and codes wherever they take us, dependant on which culture we're in.

To some degree the moral relativists have a point. They are right to say independent moral facts do not exist and that morality evolved as a useful thing to have in society. But this is where the work of Neuroscientist and Philosopher Sam Harris comes into play. In 'The Moral Landscape', Harris intends to debunk the idea that science and rationality have nothing to say about morality, and along with showing religious and spiritual ideas about morality to be invalid he also has to counter the relativist idea that there are no facts to be found in morality[20] which so many scientists tend to believe. Harris sees conscious creatures as the subjects morality refers to, and his further claim is that the concept of 'wellbeing' captures all that we can intelligibly value morally. 'Morality' — whatever people's associations with this term happen to be — really relates to the intentions and behaviours that affect the wellbeing of conscious creatures[21].

Harris is not blind to the ideas of evolution[22] and the social development of morality that moral relativism is built on. What Harris goes on to state with his theory of morality as the wellbeing of conscious creatures is that it doesn't matter how it evolved, those things that are known to be worse for the wellbeing of conscious creatures are immoral. This makes sense with what we know morality to be in society, and quite possibly quashes the individually-liberalist ideal of assigning morality a 'relativist status' to be respected regardless of what it entails. But his ideas are open to all number of problems before they can do this. Relativism is an intuitive idea once we understand the evolutionary role of morality, so are Harris' ideas defensible? I will examine what are, in my mind at least, the two main criticisms of Harris' ideas, as I believe he has currently formulated our best attempt at explaining an objective, scientific form of morality to this point.

Moral realism

Harris states his support of moral realism loud and clear: 'While moral realism and consequentialism have both come under pressure in philosophical circles, they have the virtue of corresponding to many of our intuitions about how the

---

[20] *The Moral Landscape*, Sam Harris

[21] *The Moral Landscape*, page 32-33.

[22] Harris is the founder of Project Reason, one of the popularly known 'Four Horseman of the anti-apocalypse' and writes variously about the problems with religion and non-scientific accounts of 'creation'. He's a strong voice for evolution.

world works.'[23] He goes on to state his agreement with consequentialism[24], noting it to be the under-pinning of most moral theory (including religion, which he is fiercely critical of). He also talks of how it doesn't make sense to speak of morality in any way without ascribing moral realism in the sense of consequentialism. Yet at any point does Harris get over the problems with classic moral realism (as explained earlier in this chapter that moral facts don't appear to actually exist)?

I don't believe he does. Harris still appears to be trapped in the problem of admitting that he is just assuming that the moral fact relating to 'wellbeing' exists. Will we find this moral fact while studying the ground under rocks? No. Will we be able to imply its existence when examining the issue like with the laws of quantum mechanics? No. In fact the only thing backing up our intuitions that these moral facts simply exist independently is just that: our intuitions. The idea that morality simply *is* defined as wellbeing, and thus is righteous, because we say so. And we can hardly take the same position Harris does on the absurdity of religion (that it's only supported by culturally ingrained intuitions) if we don't extend that to the absurdity of any made up, but desired facts like those he identifies in morality. If such ideas don't appear to exist, we should be honest about it.

'Is' implies 'ought'

The other issue Harris faces, and like so many others seems to fail to answer fully, comes in the form of the 'is-ought problem'. Harris' argument is essentially that it makes no sense to talk of morality as anything else but to do with

---

[23] *The Moral Landscape*, page 62.
[24] Consequentialism is defined by the Stanford Encyclopedia of Philosophy as "the view that normative properties depend only on consequences." What Harris means, in layman terms, is that there could be no moral fact which entailed worse overall consequences for sentient individuals – as ethics is about their wellbeing. On Harris' view, morality is about consequences and not just principles. A minority of moral views state that it is principles and not consequences which we should be interested in, and understandably this appears to be dying out – as Harris states, even religions at some point are consequentialist, by judging the perceived spiritual consequences of an action to be what we should be interested in.

maximising the 'wellbeing' of conscious creatures. And as such there isn't any reason why science cannot develop a branch of morality to do this, by examining the effects of behaviours and activities, and deeming them immoral based on their effect as concluded by scientific investigation.

There is much to be said of Harris's attempt, especially the latter part of noting that just because science may not be able to judge an activity as immoral now does not mean science doesn't work as a theory of morality. There are many things science doesn't know, but it doesn't mean we should abandon it in favour of accepting hearsay or spiritual justifications for truth instead, as I argued earlier. However the answer he provides to the is-ought problem does not fall into the positive aspects of the theory.

The problem itself can be explained fairly simply: just because Harris correctly identifies *how* morality is currently defined, it doesn't mean that morality *should* therefore be taken as factual. Indeed, Harris himself admits there are plenty of things we currently allow for which are immoral (the case in point being religious dogmatism). Proof, if proof were needed, that the status of things doesn't imply their justification.

If someone were to successfully create a defensible theory of morality, able to marry itself with scientific reality, then both of these issues would need to be addressed before it could be taken seriously. As previously noted, I believe Harris' attempt is the best we currently have, and yet these two criticisms stop it from even getting off the ground. We are currently a long way from a rational morality at this stage.

RATIONAL. IRRATIONAL. NON-RATIONAL. THE PROBLEM IN A NUTSHELL.

A rationalist friend of mine argues (and summarises the position very nicely) that we must draw a clear difference between what is rational and what is irrational, but also what is non-rational. Things like religion, or other 'woo' ideas like Karmic energy or psychic powers that are disproved by rational examination, are irrational notions which should not form part of understood facts or scientific knowledge. The argument goes that we must draw a difference between irrational ideas and things like morality which are not *irrational* but *non-rational*.

This is a distinction many academics seem keen to make, many rationally inclined moral theorists would agree with, and is one that moral realism seems to be heavily based on. Yet, rationally speaking, there is no reason to draw a distinction between the irrational and the non-rational at all. We can't be sure independent moral facts exist to the same degree that we can't be sure God exists. Indeed, if we were to survey people as to their base reason why it is necessary to act morally, one may find that there are as many people (if not more) who act morally from fear of divine punishment as from belief in 'non-rational' moral facts. This wouldn't be important, of course, as we know that people can delude themselves en masse. Entire societies can be based on irrational beliefs and entire moral codes can be formed around persuasive delusions. So the fact that so many people believe in independent moral facts does nothing to allay the obvious problems with them.

The problem for rational moral realists, though, is in answering the question of why exactly moral facts are non-rational, whilst religious facts are irrational (if anything is irrational, religious facts are). We know that in every other area of truth, no matter how abstract our facts get, we can link them back to direct and provable observations of reality–known as evidence. With morality there is only one link back to reality–the link back to our intuitions. Moral realism essentially thus believes that it is our intuitions that are pointing to moral facts. Yet religious people say the same thing. Indeed anyone can claim just about any nonsense is 'non-rational', and indeed many spiritualist profiteers do. If we began indulging this idea of the non-rational into other areas of life, we'd soon come a cropper; vaccinations wouldn't have to pass tests, or in Britain we could cut our spending on the National Health Service by claiming that non-rational facts show that fewer people will become ill this year. Non-rational facts shown by the prime ministers intuitions about how well his policies are going, perhaps.

There is no reason to differentiate between the irrational and the non-rational, and as far as we can see the distinction is drawn only because there is currently no understood way to ground morality in science. This is a problem. If all we have is our intuitions, and therefore we have to make assumptions about the truth values of our intuitions like we don't with science, then there is no reason to consider morality objective. In essence, if all we have is the non-rational, then all we have is the irrational, and the moral relativists are correct that there are no objective truths about morality. Yet I believe there is a way in which we can justify viewing morality as objective.

2. A Rational Solution

What should be intuitive by this point, and indeed what society is rapidly beginning to think, is that morality isn't grounded in a factual, provable way like religion or spirituality might have us believe. There are no moral facts hiding under rocks, or being implied by the study of triangles, etc. In fact with relation to rational analysis, current moral theory is shown to be wanting. Indeed, I am not the first person to notice this weakness in moral philosophy; the philosopher John Mackie (in particular) had written arguments very similar to those in the last chapter before I was even born.[25] Presumably his, and many other similar arguments, stay largely in the dark among moral philosophers for fear of what they might logically entail. The remaining issue is exactly on that subject: can we reliably show morality to objectively exist at all?

Before I argue that we can, let's make note that a rational theory of morality must take into account three important points.

a) Science is a fine way of determining truth. We need to be able to provide evidence and rationale in order to attribute facts. If morality is to be factual, it needs to be scientifically viable in the same way other science is.

b) Morality cannot exist upon fantastical notions of independent moral truths. These are unscientific.

c) The state of morality as it is, or more succinctly of wellbeing as the current marker of morality, does not by itself provide justification for morality to continue as it is.

If nothing else, what I have done so far is provide support for these ideas and it's from here that I'll formulate a solution to the problem of marrying reality with morality. Please, before

---

[25] *Ethics: Inventing Right and Wrong.* J. L. Mackie. 1977. Mackie believed, as the title of his book suggests, that we need to invent ethics as they do not exist independently. Mackie and I are in agreement on this, at least to some degree.

reading further, assume this blank slate case of morality as stated above. Drop your pre-conceptions and personal beliefs about God, moral facts formed by intuition, etc. Drop everything except the facts: that morality evolved as a social matter, that altruism is extremely useful in a developed society and that morality doesn't appear to exist outside societies of sentient individuals. It's from here that a theory of morality can be rationally invoked.

Is 'OUGHT' THE RIGHT WAY TO THINK ABOUT MORALITY?

We saw in the first chapter that an 'is' doesn't justify an 'ought'; the way things are does not tell us how they should be. Harris falls foul of this, and yet one of the positive aspects of his theory is that he states ought is a relatively unimportant term compared to the status it receives in moral theory. Perhaps he has a point. We live in a world where we can be scientifically assured that free will is largely mythical, as determinism shows us how at no point are our actions the cause of a personal spirit or soul, but rather are the effect of our genes and our experiences; none of which can be traced to any sort of 'fault' on our parts[26]. We didn't choose our genes and we didn't choose the initial experiences which led our lives to where we are today (see chapter 7 for a fuller description of determinism and free will). At no point could we realistically have chosen otherwise, given who we were at those times. As such, the notion of ought seems a little misguided, and as Harris states, 'this notion of ought is an artificial and needlessly confusing way to think about moral choice. In fact it seems to be another dismal product of Abrahamic religion'[27]. To a degree, Harris is right. We are not

---

[26] Many still argue that scientifically supported ideas like determinism are compatible with us having free will. However there is no proof that this is the case. There is as much evidence that rocks have free will as humans do. We are simply highly evolved apes; there's nothing special about us that takes us out-with the basic scientific discovery of cause and effect. If you are still in doubt with regards to how free will does not exist, please suspend disbelief until chapter 7 where the subject is discussed more fully.
[27] *The Moral Landscape,* p 38.

responsible for our actions in a strict "we could have chosen otherwise" respect, so we must take notions of ought not in their classic sense of defining what is worthy of blame and praise, but merely as a guide to our behaviour. We still, however, need a justification for ought statements in order to describe aspects of rightness and wrongness. Rightness and wrongness refer to things we ought do or not do, so the connection is a necessary one. One can disagree with the historical or classic philosophical sense of the word, but one can't disagree with the fundamentally necessary concept. For morality to be anything other than relative, ought rules must be formulated—morality is all about 'oughts' and 'ought nots', and without justifying their use we have no reason to imply morality exists. Oughts cannot be assumed for the same reason that Gods cannot.

Harris lets us further into his insight as to what morality really is with his comments in the next chapter, 'We must build our better selves into our laws, tax codes, and institutions. Knowing that we are generally incapable of valuing two children more than either child alone, we must build a structure that reflects and enforces our deeper understanding of human wellbeing.'[28] Here Harris is making the point that we perhaps do not intuitively know what is right (and in marketing campaigns we are shown to irrationally give more concern to the suffering of one individual child than to two[29]) but of more relevance here is that he shows how the essence of morality is not so much about discovering what we ought to do, so much as figuring out what we could all do to increase the wellbeing of conscious creatures. He doesn't say why one should care about conscious creatures other than oneself in the first place though, so still falls foul of the is-ought problem despite trying to valiantly redefine it.

---

[28] *The Moral Landscape*, p 70.
[29] Harris references Slovic, P. (2007). "If I look at the mass I will never act": Psychic numbing and genocide. *Judgement and Decision Making*, 2(2), 79-95.

In part, of course, Harris is right to claim classic notions of ought are flawed. But that isn't to say we don't need an ought to guide behaviour; one that morality could therefore be drawn from, and one that could be factually identified. All Harris still appears to be doing is drawing an ought from an is. No matter how greatly we criticise the classic conceptions of ought, this is still logically invalid. Yes, we do define morality as being about the wellbeing of sentient individuals, but why *ought* we care about morality in the first place? We can't very well discard the idea of religion, fairies and karma as unscientific if we are clinging to morality on the very same assertion that we simply want to pretend it's real. Morality needs a scientific backing. Harris appears to be knocking on the right doors, but not quite opening them.

FINDING AN OUGHT

Finding an 'ought' from an 'is' has perplexed philosophers for centuries, most famously in the work of David Hume in the 18th Century. We can be assured that we can't derive any justifiable ought from any naturally existing fact about the world.

However, human society has gone well beyond 'naturally existing' situations. Thus, quite simply, we solve the is-ought problem if we can identify a societal situation in which an ought can be logically derived. So, if we were all to agree that we want there to be a moral code, and we can all agree upon a rough definition of morality (such as 'morality is about maximising the wellbeing of sentient individuals'), then we can use these 'is' facts to formulate moral 'ought' facts. This is the only way around the is-ought problem, as we have created a situation in which an ought (moral code) can be derived from an is (agreement that we all want a form of moral code). A collective foundational agreement allows for a collective, objective form of morality.

Still, the idea of 'inventing' a moral code like this has many more nuances in order to become rational and not merely arbitrary; we have solved the is-ought problem, but that is all so far. If we want there to exist a form of morality which is objective and which can be studied as such, then we need to take steps which can be summarised as follows:

1) Majority societal agreement that we want there to be an objective theory of morality in the first place. Either we want to disagree with ideas like murder, rape and other acts we view as heinous, or we don't. If we want to cast such ideas as fundamentally immoral, then we need to agree that objective morality should be something which we 'invent' and stick by.

2) Once agreed, we have to work with our best definition of what morality actually is, as the foundation to extend moral laws from. Harris has provided us with an idea that it is about the wellbeing of sentient individuals. Whilst such a definition will always be open to advancement, it makes sense to stick with fair, rational conceptions. I'll argue throughout the book what I believe to be the core areas/ideas inherent in a rational theory of morality, but as yet Harris seems to have hit home with his initial definition.

3) Once defined and agreed, the subject should be handed over to science. Science is the best method that we have of determining truth and rationally extending ideas, whilst also our best method of eliminating bias, unfairness and cheating. If morality is to be viewed as truly objective, and we've already agreed that we want it to be so, then it simply has to become a science in which answers are based on and answerable to evidence rather than opinion. Not taking this important final step means we are answering the is-ought problem without taking rational morality onto its logical conclusions. If we aren't taking the logical conclusions, then we aren't pushing forth with the solution of the is-ought problem, which was about agreeing to a definition of morality *rationally*. We feed back into an ever increasing loop of error.

A GUIDING 'OUGHT' PRINCIPLE?

By following the steps above, we can carve a rational theory of morality which is objective and not relative. The last step – handing morality over to science – is the most important part, as it means morality has to at least comply with the rules of science and not be arbitrarily extended. But in order to do this moral science can only make one basic assumption, just as other science can: that we *ought to be rational*. In other words, we set the foundational principle that morality is about maximising the wellbeing of sentient individuals and then we devote ourselves to being rational, and only rational, about extending it.

This assumption of rationality is at the bottom of every science: we have to be as rational as we can, testing experience and anecdote to develop ideas and truths which we can replicate and explain. If we develop a theory of morality with only one guiding rule – that we ought to be rational – there seems no reason why we can't have an objective, scientific theory of morality. We follow the three steps, mentioned previously, to create a science of morality, and then we retain a guiding principle that we ought to be rational.

This kind of rational 'ought' principle is also not so much an assumption to make regarding morality, so much as an assumption we implicitly make regarding everything. Science is based on it, our minds work in a way which strives for it (indeed beliefs can't stick with anyone without them believing the belief, which is a rational system. People don't believe things in spite of believing them, which would be truly irrational). We ought to be rational if we want the truth – something science has known since its primitive foundations. And just as rationality shows classic theories of morality to be lacking, it shows that rationality is the only assumption morality can make if it wants to be scientific.

WHY DOES A RATIONAL MORALITY NEED TO BE OBJECTIVE, OR SCIENCE-BASED?

A clear objection will be the positing of why I think this three step idea of creating moral science is any more truthful or scientific than a relativist form of morality. This is an important question, as the answer hits right on the issue of why moral science (as a consensually, societally agreed type) is desperately necessary. Relativist logic assumes that because morality is a certain way (i.e., it evolved relatively) we should thus view it that way. That's only true in one sense: we should not ignore facts about the evolution of morality by stating, like spiritual accounts of morality do, that moral facts exist in our intuitions or our hearts. However science certainly does not say that we *should* do that which science tells us we can. Richard Dawkins suffered this kind of uninformed criticism with his publishing of The Selfish Gene in 1976. He was the subject of many liberal accusations that he was justifying selfish, conservative politics by stating that we consist of selfish genes. The criticism failed to notice that just because scientific fact tells us we are a certain way, or in this case that our genes are a certain way, does not mean that we ought to act that way.

And this is where a theory of rational morality becomes necessary. Relativism can account perfectly well for why morality exists, but it is not rational unless one ignores the is-ought problem.

So we are rationally justified in going above relativism and creating something objective. But in order for it to be truly objective, it also needs to be part of a collective method that strives for objectivity; and the only human method that does this in any meaningful way is organised science. Once, as described in the first two steps, we have a foundation for a theory (a societally agreed one) we simply need to throw the one scientific assumption in: that we ought to be rational. We then have an incredibly useful blueprint, and also an incredibly simple one, of determining moral facts based upon a set moral principle (that we ought to be rational) in relation to a foundational definition which we are being rational about. Just like physics asks us to be rational about our observations in physics experiments, moral science asks us to be rational about causing the better wellbeing for sentient individuals in moral experiments (which occur daily in our lives) due to this being a basic moral principle which we all agree with.

A DIFFERENT TYPE OF SCIENCE: APPROACHING THE NUANCES OF THE THEORY

There's no doubt that the types of facts we are dealing with in morality are fundamentally different — facts in physics are true whether you believe them or not, or whether humans exist or not, whereas moral facts are more socially grounded — they are relative to our species, perhaps, and could theoretically change based on values. This is not relativity in the way moral relativism suggests, e.g. that morality is just what exists to guide the society. Entire cultures could still be less developed than others in moral terms (by explicitly creating less wellbeing for sentient individuals), in the same way that entire cultures can be less developed in health-care terms. Rather the relative notion of scientific morality relates to changes of a more elementary level; ie, if we begin valuing pain rather than pleasure, the moral facts will look a great deal different to how they look now that we value pleasure and want to avoid pain. The facts of morality are entirely dependent on certain fundamental values, as fundamental values determine what wellbeing consists of. [30] In this sense, and this sense only, moral science is relative.

We also can't make the same claims about independent moral facts and physics facts: the claim that 'killing is wrong' is not of the same truth value as 'gravity is the force that pulls us to Earth'. Strong evidence would be needed to disprove

---

[30] This is certainly an area for further study, in order to flesh out a more universal/meta-physical idea of what this kind of morality entails, how we decide which values are important and deserving of different rules, and which are simply cultural errors. However in this book I will stick to the simpler topic of moral theory in this world, with human beings of the type who currently exist.

either, but we can imagine situational evidence where the first statement is shown to be incorrect (i.e., killing in self-defence, or where the choice is between two deaths), whereas evidence to disprove the latter is not currently available. But this difference in status also doesn't mean we should claim moral truths are simply relative. Sure, there are some elements of relativity to science (let's remember that a perfectly straight line on Earth is curved when viewed from space, and understanding this type of relativity of perspective is important), but we don't claim it is relative depending on the society that invented it. Physics exists because it is useful and morality exists because it is useful. They still each have objective truths, as I will argue they must.

If we can choose to create a scientific theory of morality, we can choose to create a scientific theory of anything. Rational morality doesn't exist.

Morality is different from other science (admittedly) in the respect that we would be choosing to make it science, in a way we wouldn't have to with physical science. With physics or biology, for example, we are observing phenomena and studying them, thus discovering truths about the physical world which we can subject to tests and evidence. Whereas with morality we are deciding it to be rational, based on an agreed need and foundation, and then subjecting the whole concept to scientific and rational discourse. So the criticism might ask 'if we can choose to make morality a science, why can't we choose to make anything else a science?' A science of homeopathy, perhaps?

Homeopathy is a form of alternative 'medical' treatment whereby, depending on the illness, a patient will receive a water solution with an impossibly small amount of a certain active ingredient dissolved in it as a cure. In scientific tests, homeopathy is shown to work no better than a placebo (placebos themselves are scientifically much more interesting than fake cures like homeopathic treatments provide, but that's another story[31]) and there's good reason for that; the amount of active ingredient in homeopathic treatments is so small that we are talking a ratio of less than one drop in the entirety of the world's oceans. These treatments are placebos, scientifically speaking, but the practitioners activate the placebo effect especially well by giving the patients time, care and a garble of pseudo-science regarding the treatment itself. This is the placebo effect done in the most deceptive, but intelligent of ways. Unsurprisingly, many in the scientific community are up in arms regarding this treatment and the problems it causes for the understanding of science in society, as well as the irrational nature of governments spending millions on these cures which can be shown to not work.

So why can't we choose to make homeopathy a science? Firstly, ideas like homeopathy are anti-science. They are made up ideas that try to deceive our human capabilities. If we were to be honest and scientific about homeopathy, we couldn't back them in the way we can back rational morality (ie, we'd immediately fall foul of our own scientific assumption that *we ought to be rational*). Homeopathy only works because of the placebo effect and the ignorance of the lack of science behind it. The idea that we ought to be rational directly opposes a science of homeopathy, so such an idea is dead in the water before we start; we can't have a scientific theory of homeopathy for the same reason we can't have a scientific theory of fairies. If we could show that homeopathy was good for human wellbeing, with few if any negative effects, then we would have an argument for justifying it (though not for making it a science, as societally agreeing to make a placebo a science – like we have to with morality –

---

[31] We need turn no further than the first resource linked, *Bad Science*, for yet further explanation on this (the book reads like an introductory course in scientific method for those of us who are not scientists by trade). Placebos have been found to be effective on a sliding scale, whereby the more dramatic an intervention, the more effective the placebo is at curing the ailment. For instance, one sugar pill is more effective than two sugar pills, an injection is more effective still, and even more dramatic interventions like perceived surgery can claim to have even better results, when in all three cases nothing medicinal is actually done. These are not anecdotally posited ideas, they are scientifically supported and they reveal a great deal about the way to view illness.

would ruin the effects of the placebo). However there are huge moral problems with it anyway. I will not delve into details here, but is it safe to be confusing people with scientific sounding ideas which are really bunk, but telling them its science? Especially in a society where so many distrust science, and fail to understand it? Similarly, how safe is it to ask people to throw their faith behind a cure that doesn't work—even if the placebo effect accompanying it cures this small medical issue—and risk them refusing genuine medical treatment in the future due to this reliance and faith in pseudo-science? And finally, is it really good for people to be of the type that they throw their support behind things that they don't understand, based on the acceptance of authority? Sure we need authority figures often, but with science and technology people could delve into the reasons why these things work if they really want to (or at least grasp them slightly), whereas homeopathy asks them to suspend their rational abilities and instincts in favour of full blown faith. All of these issues, among others, would need solving before we even considered homeopathy a useful method, let alone consider debauching the tried and tested method of science by intentionally deceiving entire societies with a science of homeopathy.

A more difficult criticism of rational morality might be found in picking a more rationally able topic: 'why can't we create a scientific theory of basketball?' Well, we can! There's an awful lot of science used in basketball, and if there is public need to create one then we should begin institutionalising it. I firmly believe there is more need for a science of morality, as I believe it's more important to deal with death, suffering and wellbeing than with playing a sport better or more effectively than someone else, but this is just my opinion and thus is open to analysis. There is no reason there couldn't be a science of basketball though and sports scientists exist exactly for these reasons. What do you think coaches of basketball teams do, for example? They try to objectively find ways to be better than their opponents, which will reflect in the victory within the rules of the game. This is, in a very real sense, an amateur attempt at basketball science.

An even more challenging criticism would be one that picked a subject with conceptually exact similarity to morality: 'if we can create a scientific theory of morality, why can't we create a scientific theory of what are objectively the best colours?' This one is more difficult to answer, but essentially is a mix between the basketball and homeopathy versions of the question. Like with basketball, I am open to admitting 'we can' if we find reason for creating a 'science of the best colours', but then what evidence are you going to use? There doesn't seem to be any basis, like there is for morality. We know about the uses of colours, the psychological effects, etc, but we don't know anything about why one colour would be better than another, or what 'better' would even be referring to when it comes to colours. Whereas morality is important to human civilisation, being a rationally evolved concept, favourite colours appear to be only a personal preference, with most people harbouring no strong feelings at all.

My feelings on why morality differs from colour are down to the importance to civilisation. I mean, perhaps within human society one can decipher reasons for judging a person's favourite colour wrong, based on the rational nature of having a favourite colour. I can't, but one day someone might be able to. At this stage, I can't envision such a science needing to come to the foreground, as I can't imagine on what grounds majority societal opinion will have cause or reason for agreeing that such a science is necessary though. Raising a similarity between favourite colours and morality is conceptually acceptable (both are abstract ideas which we would need to explicitly make into science) but historically and referentially ridiculous. It is the difference between practical, real world science and theoretical philosophy.

So why can we decide to make morality rational? The answer is a split between rational analysis (which differentiates it from the science of homeopathy) and civilizational importance (which differentiates it from basketball and colours). If we consensually agree that morality is important, and it needs to be neutral (and by definition morality does need to be neutral and fair, as that's what morality is), then logic is begging us to do two things:

1) Admit that none of us implicitly have sacred knowledge about morality which we can pass onto each other; there are no 'moral facts' that exist independent of human culture for us to learn.

2) Create a socially constructed science of morality instead. Sociology also doesn't exist out-with human culture and yet we have a whole area of academia studying and making progress in it. It split from subjects like philosophy and thrives on scientific method. There is no reason why morality can't do this too.

In a nutshell, this brief piece of reasoning on 'why morality, but not...' should soothe many of the philosophical issues with an idea like rational morality. How it leaves philosophers feeling (morality being the last real form of truth finding which is granted to philosophy over science, in my opinion) is another matter, for another book. There is no doubt, though, that morality should be a science when we look at it rationally.

WHY OUGHT WE BE RATIONAL?

The fact that we ought to be rational is one already accepted by all forms of scientific investigation and is the one form of experiment and truth which is already respected by everyone in society. It is the one basic assumption all scientific endeavours make and that all people value no matter how much they claim not to: they wouldn't be doing *anything* without it[32]. As long as a moral theory doesn't make any assumptions other than that we ought to be rational, then it is scientifically viable.

If we doubt that we ought to be rational, in order to find what is right or what is true, then we are creating a paradox for ourselves. Every word we speak and every idea we formulate owes itself, at some point, to rationality. Doubting that we ought to be rational misses not just *the* point, but *every* point. Every criticism of this principle itself implies the rationality that it aims to delete (by virtue of the nature of criticisms, which aim to be a rational criticism that holds intellectual water). Rationality is the study of reality. It is the observation and development of understanding about the world as it is. We therefore ought to be rational, and as objective as possible about it, if we want to discover facts about something. Doubting this is almost unintelligible. It is not a societally agreed moral ought that makes the propositions true, but rather it is a logical necessity for truth finding; if one isn't being rational in their endeavours, then one isn't doing any more than finding subjective truth. Positing an 'ought to be rational' when truth finding is like positing an 'ought to be truth finding' when truth finding. It's a logical necessity.

Rationality is as close to an ought as one can get in moral theory, and the ought involved is one of a profoundly different type to the ought that one might claim to exist 'to be compassionate' or 'to be kind'. Claiming we ought to do anything *but* be rational is to make an assumption that one can't justify (which is unfortunately something that moral philosophers have a rich history of). Claiming we ought to be

---

[32] A person will always act rationally in some basic sense. No matter how spiritually inclined, they are always making decisions as conscious subjects of a life. It is impossible for human beings to decide to do things 'randomly', and were we to have a perfect understanding of human behaviour and every effect on a person's mind, we would in fact be able to predict a person's next thought, action or decision. We might never genuinely have these kinds of technological capabilities, just like we may never have perfect capabilities for predicting the behaviour for other primates, but this doesn't mean our actions could ever be irrational as a systematic matter.

rational, however, is perfectly justifiable if we want to engage in any form of discussion about morality in the first place. As mentioned previously, it is a logical necessity. Kindness or compassion might be rational responses in certain situations (and so might be derived as 'ought rules' from the principle of rationality in certain situations), but they aren't provable, or anything more than personally preferable principles. Whereas an obligation to be rational is necessary before we even start to communicate an idea. As assumptions go, rationality is the basis of everything: a self-proving assumption that one can rely on.

Before going any further, let's test this theory of rational morality by the three factors put forth at the beginning of the chapter to make sure it is sound.

a) Science is a fine way of determining truth. We need to be able to provide evidence and rationale in order to attribute facts. If morality is to be factual, it needs to be scientifically viable in the same way other science is.

Being rational is the preserve of science and is the holy grail of scientific investigation. If one can rationally show their idea to be true having taken into account all the evidence for and against, then the idea can be said to be true. Thus our guiding principle that *'we ought to be rational'* sits perfectly well with point a). Rationality is the only base assumption in science, so taking it on board to create a branch of science concerned with morality is logical. Indeed, making other assumptions seems baseless, but making this assumption is necessary for understanding anything and everything.

Many would criticise this by claiming that science makes several assumptions, not just that of rationality. This argument takes a couple of different paths in modern conversation. One is the argument that scientists make inherent assumptions in order to prove experiments: assumptions such as 'phenomena can be understood', or 'physical laws are the same everywhere'. But even if a scientist is throwing her faith behind these extra assumptions (we could call them 'second order assumptions'), they are still either open to change (given new evidence) or else backed by the deeper assumption that we ought to be rational. The latter is often the true answer, as these second order assumptions are tested and shown to be evident time and time again, so the rational instinct can take them as true until proven otherwise. It is rational for her to make these assumptions based on this justified reasoning.

The other form of the argument is that scientists must explicitly assume things about the validity of their observations, or validity of observation as a method at all. The claim here seems slightly deeper than the previous one, in claiming to show that science has more than one first order assumption. But again, any assumption like those claimed here is tested and subjected to evidence also. The truth is that there may be an awful lot of ideas which scientists learn, and thus take for granted (or as it is more commonly known 'assume') when doing science, but that is because science in general works. They have no need to test each assumption in every experiment (whether it be about the validity of their observations, or the nature of physical laws) as both the historical experience of other scientists, as well as things like observations demonstrably working and not returning unexpected error, already examines and tests those assumptions implicitly. Even when these assumptions are undermined, they are changed, so this shows the assumption was not fundamental in the first place.

In situations where second order assumptions are changed it is that single first order assumption (we ought to be rational) that changes them. There are many famous examples of these second order assumptions changing throughout history: the switching from an assumption about the Earth being at the centre of the solar system, scientists increasing the number of known elements and perhaps most famously the discovery of behaviour at particle level. These changes in turn demonstrate further evidence in favour of science accepting rationality implicitly, and also evidence that these other second order assumptions are not assumptions of science but rather are part of the body of knowledge which science consists of (which is discovered and developed, rather than assumed). The only constant that has remained is the guiding principle that we ought to be rational.

We might say that within individual experiments a scientist is assuming the usefulness of repetition, or the validity of isolating variables, or perhaps even the advantages of thoroughly noting the method. As a matter of explicit assumptions within individual tests, it is fair to say that scientists are assuming a great deal. But each of these assumptions is backed by every piece of scientific investigation that takes place and so, as a fundamental matter of the nature and philosophy of science, it is demonstrably true that the only true assumption that science makes is regarding rationality. And in truth, even rationality is only assumed because each and every methodologically successful experiment (whether the results were successful or not) or scientific advancement justifies this single assumption. Science is a strong method of truth finding, whilst rationality is, for good reason, its only foundational principle.

b) Morality cannot exist upon fantastical notions of independent moral truths. These are unscientific.

As noted, rationality is a scientific assumption. 'We ought to be rational' is the base assumption that science makes, indeed it is the basic assumption everyone makes. (Even spiritual arguments are defended by rational claims, i.e., "God *must* exist". No one truly thinks God doesn't exist, but truly believes in him anyway; one can claim this, but belief cannot work in an irrational way like this.) One might argue that it's a fantastical notion to suggest that we ought to be rational, but as already shown, this criticism is flawed. It seems to me that to speak meaningfully about anything, and to create concepts about anything, we need to evoke one basic assumption of rationality being a meaningful, desired term. Even the notion that 'we ought to be rational is a fantastical notion' already accepts the fact that it is trying to be critical of, in order to criticise it. After all, the criticism is striving to be a *rational* one (and were its propositions correct, it would be one). The formulation of the very argument that 'we have no reason to be rational' involves a rational argument itself, so how much sense does it really make to doubt the importance of rationality as a base 'ought'? We are not talking about a moral necessity to embrace an 'ought to be rational', remember, but rather a truth-finding necessity; one cannot justify independent moral claims with this assumption, but one *can* justify independent truth finding claims with it. And science already has justified the need for rationality. So making it the only guiding principle in a theory of rational morality creates a logical simplicity.

However, as a result of the paradoxical critique that we *needn't* be rational, some might feel no need to accept the argument that we ought to be rational and feel no need to formulate a rational critique of it. As if being *irrational* is a get out clause that allows one to not accept rationality as a base assumption. Again, this is still grasping at rational straws. It only makes sense to choose to be irrational as an antidote to the value of rationality, if one is already assuming that they need to make a rational argument. Or, to put it simpler, if X says rationality is important and Z disagrees — thereby feeling obligated to act as irrationally as possible to prove X incorrect — then Z is trying to behave in a way which is rationally consistent with her opinion about the unimportance of rationality. This shows that rationality is so necessary for human behaviour that even the most far-fetched of thought experiments still show human beings as quintessentially striving for it.

In summary, everything, including science, needs to make one assumption to begin investigating truth. Science, as noted above, makes the strong case for the assumption being that we ought to be rational. We can't even argue this assumption without accepting it, which makes it out to be a strong idea. Further assumptions above *we ought to be rational,* which allow for the irrational (like independent moral facts) violate the first assumption, so are flawed. This is keen, logical claims making.

c) The state of morality as it is, or more succinctly of wellbeing as the current marker of morality, does not by itself provide justification for morality to continue as it is.

My claim that we ought to be rational makes no assumption that morality is a certain way and so is right. In fact, although we make all of our decisions based on some form of intention to be rational (show me someone whose brain works by not formulating decisions and I'll admit error here), most of our moral decisions could arguably be improved if we actually made the decision to extend external rational analysis and consistency to them, like we do in science.

In any case, the theory that one ought to be rational is not assuming anything about morality as it currently is, it's only assuming what good truth finding *already* assumes, then assigning that same method to morality. It only asks that if morality is to be objective, we need to invent or agree on the basic principles of a morality in the first place. Undoubtedly these will involve wholesale changes from our current opinion-based moral guide.

HOW CAN AN OBLIGATION TO BE RATIONAL LEAD TO A DECENT FORM OF MORALITY?

It's easy to show why rationality is both an inbuilt system for human beings and a necessary one. Hence why supposing 'we ought to be rational' is a sensible scientific assumption. We stunt the growth of every form of truth finding without it. It is also relatively easy to create the conditions that allow us to draw an ought from an is. However showing rationality to be a good way of judging morality in reality, when it has been disregarded as such throughout history, is quite a way more difficult. In fact prejudice against rationality as a marker of morality is rife. And yet so long as we have agreed on a definition of morality which we want and which holds up to analysis, then rationality is a perfect tool for making moral decisions.

What it means to accept the obligation to be rational is thus to admit this, but also (in my opinion) Harris' entirely rational claim that morality refers only to the wellbeing of conscious individuals. It makes no sense for us to value trees, mountains or oceans if the wellbeing of conscious individuals is not at stake. Morality doesn't refer to trees, or physical facts, but rather to the wellbeing of individuals who can experience what happens to them. This is a rational definition of morality.

This does not mean that to be rational we simply need to accept current moral rules, like a moral relativist would, under the guise that these rules have evolved to work and thus are rational. This is not so much rational as ignorant and it falls foul of the third point which any rational theory of morality must oppose (point c: that morality being a certain way doesn't justify its continuance in this way). We must accept, perhaps, Harris' definition of morality (unless we can better it) but we don't necessarily have to accept the way things are; to do this would be to act unscientifically and violate the 'ought to be rational' which we've already established is the *only* moral rule which works. Take physics, for example. We find facts in physics in one society, yet if another group elsewhere shows those facts to be wrong and new ones to be correct, then those facts must change in *all* societies. Societies that are aware but don't change are wrong. A rational theory of morality must go on to accept a definition of morality, like Harris provides, to be correct until evidenced agreement can imply its incorrectness. From this base even the most culturally ingrained of acts could be scientifically shown wrong as a moral matter. Moral rules derive from rational deductions leading from a general principle about the wellbeing of all conscious individuals.

But also pragmatically, to look back just 100, or even 50 years is to look back and see western society in a worse place for women, people of colour and those in lower social classes, so to state that where we are now is better and thereby perfectly rational and riskless, is arrogant and historically ignorant. Irrational on a basic analysis, even. Indeed, speaking of the conscious species of human beings alone, the incidence of religious fundamentalist terrorism, right wing political ignorance of non-white non-males and a growing gap between the poorest and richest (funded by a growing category of the poorest) should tell us that this isn't the best world we could manage and that it is still incredibly risky and irrational for all of us. It takes a fairly irrational ignorance of inequality to sum up that morality is working the best it could, even when we ignore sentient individuals other than humans.

It's rational to extend our current morality to the greatest number, and to the greatest forms of equality, and that seems to hold true as a pragmatic matter as well. Not fostering this wide reaching equality is simply preaching for inconsistency, for moral rules that promote explicit selfishness, and this perhaps holds vicious danger for us even without considering moral science (which asks for moral code to be extended consistently, not selfishly).

Not extending this rationally created and required morality, on the basis it might benefit us or our small groups more not to extend it, is slipping into a poor form of act-utilitarianism. (And whilst I won't go into the many problems with this position immediately, it is useful to note.[33]) Indeed even the richer, better served members of society at current are still taking risks which are by no means 'rational'. We see the gap between the rich and the poor growing and this can only be funded by a larger 'poor' group. Hence those people of power are fast diminishing their own positions of security simply in a vain attempt to get more 'security' in evolutionary terms, by creating a smaller number of targets of themselves. Yet they don't need more security; such risks are irrational (as even if protection is easily affordable, it isn't perfect) and bred from our fallible human instincts to always reach for 'more', not from some human capability to be rational (which would involve being satisfied when secure, giving excess away to allow others to be satisfied and not dangerous to you when they struggle for survival). The latter is completely

---

[33] This will be discussed in more details in chapter 4.

distinguished by such slavery to base instincts. It is not rational to listen to the greed instinct once far reaching security is reached.

The main thing to take away, though, is not the pragmatics but that we ought to be rational. If we are to believe in and use morality, then we have to treat it like science. This means not fudging results when it suits us personally (like sacrificing another conscious individual for 'more things') by appealing to personal beliefs or intentions. We ought to be rational, not selfish. These two are often confused, and this itself is an irrational extension of the idea of 'survival of the fittest': one which has no place in an informed theory of morality or science (which we can hopefully begin to see are the same thing). Rationality is about truth finding, not about getting as many things for oneself as possible. And this is also the root of the reason why rationality pragmatically works as a basis for morality.

Morality is entirely rational and has bought us to a more civilised society.[34] And civilised, productive society, as well as rational, consistent morality, both demand equality and consistency. The two things go hand in hand. The evolution of morality may have happened through self-serving interests that altruism (and therefore, morality) has evolved from in the past; however this does not mean that the rational way is to carry on viewing it in selfish terms.

PREJUDICE IS IRRATIONAL

Undoubtedly there are still unanswered objections and criticism, which I will look across in the next chapter. For now, it would be useful to look at a couple of examples of scientific

---

[34] http://www.ted.com/talks/steven_pinker_on_the_myth_of_violence.html In this talk Steven Pinker remarks that our 21st Century society produced 100 million human deaths through war and violence, however our more irrational hunter-gatherer societies (societies which are decidedly less civilised and organised) would have produced around 2 billion deaths through violence. This is a huge difference and there is no doubt that a more civilised society, even with its questionable wars, creates less violence. Pinker's recent academic work which is referenced later in the chapter is the proof for this comment.

moral code in order to get some real world ideas as to what it involves. Rule one, I suppose we could call it, is that prejudice is irrational. Prejudice is, scientifically speaking, an arbitrary deviation from rationality; the moral equivalent of someone claiming that gravity is actually just invisible strawberry jelly (i.e., a position obviously inconsistent with the basic rules of rationality, or misunderstanding the facts we already know about the subject). Indeed, one would have to be ignorant of the very meaning of morality to posit prejudice as consistent with it, so the strawberry jelly is in some ways a generous analogy by gifting prejudice, as it does, with an understanding at least of the basics of moral theory. After all, someone arguing for the strawberry jelly hypothesis must at least understand that 'stickiness' is in some way a feasible explanation for 'pull'. But prejudice is the moral science equivalent of blind bias. It is a basic scientific error that swaps consistent, useful results for random personal opinions. That's unfeasible on a basic and obvious level.

Let's also demonstrate how the pragmatic interacts with the science though (in order to show that this form of morality isn't unworkable). Prejudice has a rational basis only so far as it breeds out of our fear of difference (i.e., we might push sexism, racism, xenophobia, homophobia, etc., out of a will to protect only those who look like or seem to be like us, in an effort to protect our genes)[35]. It would be incredibly foolish to grant prejudice equal importance and thereby equal standing with equality on a pragmatic level. Prejudice leads to marginalisation and violence—I don't know anyone who would claim the western world was more civilised when racism was legally protected, or when women or people of colour could be legally owned. Indeed, there are growing

---

[35] It has been suggested to me that prejudice also plays a role in protecting power, something one might come across in a Functionalist perspective of sociology. While this may be true, it is not a conscious system – there is no boardroom of people deciding that prejudice must be upheld in order to protect their power. Rather, the utilisation of prejudice in this way is incidental and a misattribution of instincts as I discuss. It just happens to create a society where power is protected in this way.

academic arguments to show this point more objectively.[36] As morality has extended, society has become a more civilised place. Of course it has. Ridding prejudice from our moral shores is an example of rationality defeating basic instinctual ideas such as a blanket fear of outsiders. We'd welcome a conscious, mutually fulfilling, widely understood and rational morality to eliminate prejudice like this, wouldn't we? That's what would make our conscious, moral society less risky and better for us than an instinctually, more prone to error, morality of a vampire bat society. The pragmatics seem to favour rational morality again and we can't underestimate the importance of this, given that so many ignore scientific views of the world under the false assumption that it can lead to personally conceived immoral actions.

PRACTICAL APPLICATION OF THE RATIONAL

Earlier I mentioned one solution which many might perceive as valid, after such a discovery as rational morality like I put forth here, and that is of act-utilitarianism. This would go something like: *morality is about being rational, thereby we don't need universal rules as much as a case by case analysis of the rational aspects upon every decision: that would be truly rational.* I would go so far as to say this is the first intuition one might come to when taking a position that claimed to be rational morality. However there are important mistakes which show why this would be an irrational position to hold.

I earlier quoted Harris who states: "We must build our better selves into our laws, tax codes, and institutions. Knowing that we are generally incapable of valuing two children more than either child alone, we must build a structure that reflects and enforces our deeper understanding of human wellbeing." Here lies the reason why the compulsion for act-utilitarianism doesn't make sense (and

---

[36] Take a look at Steven Pinker's 'The Better Angels of our Nature' for instance, which charts the decline of violence throughout history, noting that there has never been a better time to be a potential victim. Pinker himself notes one of the reasons for this to be our escalating use of 'reason'.

also one of the reasons why, despite the obvious criticisms, I hold Harris' ideas in high regard).

A theory of rational morality, as I am explaining it, does appeal to the desire to be rational and to the basic assumption that we ought to be rational. However this does not mean that we will suddenly become rational machines ourselves, able to foresee the future and calculate all the possible outcomes in any given situation. Indeed, as also mentioned earlier, we are evolutionarily disposed to erroneous decisions about morality (such as taking on board the negative experience of one child, and giving it more attention than the experience of two, or perhaps even a million children). Fighting those errors which are hardwired into our make up almost certainly means that we need laws and rules, and rational extensions of those as a general matter.

Undoubtedly this will mean that some things are forbidden that should be allowed, or in some cases our hands might be legally tied for doing the right thing. Consider, for example, the laws regarding human murder. One might wish they were changed to allow for euthanasia, but recognise that doing so would allow the law to be left open for all manner of irresponsible acts by questionable individuals. My theory of morality states we ought to be rational, but I do not for a second foresee (as much as my ego would like to) a day when everyone has read this book, and also when no-one acts irrationally as a moral matter. Like with any science, we cannot even attest that one day we will know all the answers, so we certainly cannot be sure we will ever be able to inertly act with a perfect knowledge of them. As such, it might well be necessary to keep laws regarding murder as stringent as they are now, even if they negatively impact on the will of some to end their lives with assistance[37]. Similarly, without

---

[37] Please note that I am not saying the laws regarding murder are correct here, or that euthanasia should be made much easier. I am neither qualified nor practically informed enough to come down on either side, so it is not my place to say. I raise this as a practical example, not as a personal opinion of what should happen in either case; I apologise in advance if anyone views it as a shot against their knowledge, as that was not my intention.

laws regarding equality and fairness (which, undoubtedly, society is still a long way from perfecting) we could lose track of what is rational altogether.

I will touch more upon the practical issues and subjects we should be considering most fervently later on. But it is important to consider morality as a form of science, remember. That means we need laws, communities of moral scientists with which to peer review theories and rational analysis to create solutions to complex problems. Science doesn't work on an act-by-act basis and there is no reason to suppose that it would be better placed doing so.

WHAT DO RATIONAL MORAL FACTS LOOK LIKE?

Earlier on I was very critical of the idea of classical moral realism, particularly the idea of independent moral facts which our moral intuitions are somehow uncovering. The whole thing reeks of fantasy in the same way religious beliefs do, but I was very sure to point out that moral facts may well exist in some way.

The quote by Harris, twice linked in this chapter now, explains how we are not always good machines for distinguishing what is rational and what is not. This is never more true than when on the subject of morality, in which we have traditions and upbringings that teach us to value all kinds of moral opinions, based in all kinds of moral doctrines (whether it be law, religious literature, family tradition, societal culture, media norms, etc.). If moral facts do exist (and I believe in some sense they can), they are in the realm of rational consistency, i.e. it is objectively factual that racism is immoral, from extending our collective, rational agreements about morality; that we shouldn't be racists. This is not because there is some independent fact (similar to the type of factual statement that 'rocks are hard') which says 'racism is immoral', but rather because 'racism is immoral' is an objectively true fact, in relation to the fact that morality rationally exists and thus can be treated as a science, which in turn then has to be consistently rational. Discriminating on an arbitrary factor like race, as racism entails, would be the very opposite of rational consistency, which states that race is only a relevant criterion when it isn't arbitrary. Racism is irrational and based on arbitrary assumptions, by definition.

This may come close to a classical moral realist conception of moral facts (i.e., that it is simply true that racism is immoral), but it is important to note the difference. This fact is not judged by our intuitions, but by rationality. Moral facts do exist, but *because* of rationality, and are only based upon the assumption that we ought to be rational. Similarly, if we one day discover a society where racism can be deemed a net positive, then the negative connotations and irrational nature of racism will disappear and it may switch truth value in a profound way. Thus showing real moral facts to be essentially different to the basic classical moral realism which many philosophers espouse. Though, for the current world situation, this scientific version of moral facts is very much one and the same as a more rigid, fantastical account as far as these meta-ethics are concerned.

I briefly explained prejudice as 'rule one' of a rational theory of morality; one would posit prejudice as bias, and thus something to be avoided when deciding on moral facts. No doubt a scientific method of figuring moral facts could develop many other rules, but I sincerely believe prejudice to be the most important starter. The facts such a method would come up with might be as widely focused as 'all other things being equal, people of the same skin colour should be considered to be equal' or as narrowly focused as 'murder could never be considered morally acceptable in situation x'. Scientific investigation would have to decipher the individual facts from a full analysis of outcomes, results and effects of the issue in question; and it will likely never answer every moral quandary, in the same way that physical science will never answer every possible physical quandary. However, upon a societal adoption of rational morality, it will become clear exactly what kinds of moral facts we are looking for. Perhaps we want to decide what should be generally against the law and what shouldn't, or similarly, we might want to use evidence as to how specific we should be with individual court cases, or how standardised each legal decision should be (so as to create a consistent system of deterrence). The pragmatics of how we use rational morality – and so of what kind of statements constitute moral facts – are wide open, even if the logic and methodology of the system isn't.

We shouldn't abandon moral rules in favour of an act by act appraisal, though, as this would be extending rational morality to an irrational conclusion which posited we were perfect rational machines. Rather, we should discover and live by moral facts in the form of rationally investigated and tested ideas. We can, and indeed should, guide our behaviour based on our scientific understanding of the interests of ourselves and other sentient creatures. Moral facts should reflect the scientific understanding of what we know serves our and others' interests well, and by avoiding what we know doesn't. This practical aspect will be discussed at length in chapter 5 onwards, but is vital to mention in order to be understood now. Moral facts do not exist as most currently believe them to, in relation to our intuitions or outside our society in some way; however, it is very rational to speak of moral facts as a matter of rights, or forbidden behaviour. For example, it may well be rational to assert that it is a moral fact that unprovoked murder is wrong – an idea society already deems correct. There might be many subjects like this on which rational morality may not need to move our opinions at all, but we should certainly be open to scepticism and movement in all areas, just in case.

3. *Developing and Defending Rational Morality*

Any new idea like the one I put forth is bound to be subject to all manner of misinterpretation and criticism that is largely unfounded. We are talking about an entirely new idea and subject area — a philosophy of moral science — that is vastly unintuitive to current moral theorists, as it holds rationality as its principle. As such I believe it is my duty to examine some of this before it even begins, so in this chapter I'll briefly discuss some of the main problems which will undoubtedly surface.[38]

PEOPLE ARE UNMOVED BY RATIONALITY

There are many studies claiming to indicate that people are best moved by emotional wording or emotional accounts of immoral events than they are by hearing the rational reasons why such events are wrong. They claim to show that people are better moved by emotional ideas in general than rational ones[39]. Undoubtedly, many will state this shows a rational version of morality to be wrong.

If emotion motivates people, rationality doesn't

This is not a good criticism of what I have written, as it assumes that because rationality is the basis of morality then

---

[38] Some of the main criticisms were dealt with in the explanation of the theory in Chapter 2. For example, the problem of figuring why we ought to be rational in the first place, or why rationality means we should be moral at all. The criticisms I explain are further ideas which have been bought to my attention through discussion or contemplation on this issue.

[39] One of these was noted in the last chapter: Slovic, P. (2007). *"If I look at the mass I will never act": Psychic numbing and genocide. Judgement and Decision Making, 2(2), 79-95.* However, many studies claim to prove that either rationality isn't a good motivator, or even that rational people are less moral. Check here for some examples: http://www.hoover.org/publications/policy-review/article/6577.

emotion is no longer important. This is not what I have claimed. I have argued that traditional moral realism is wrong as it assumes the existence of independent moral facts, and that these don't exist. Thereby it is irrational to hold people to rules based around fantastical but ultimately flawed notions of morality, however well they motivate people.

Although being rational is certainly the key to uncovering the truth, this doesn't mean that emotion can't be used to advocate different moral causes. I may even believe that everyone should be trained to think rationally, perhaps having mathematical or formal logic education built in to the curriculum of the schooling system, but this does not mean that advocating with the use of emotion before this happens is wrong. It also doesn't mean that emotion is somehow unimportant; emotion being an entirely rational, evolutionarily formed occurrence. I would never argue that emotional reactions themselves are irrational, and I don't believe it could successfully be done.

What is wrong, however, is using emotion to bully people into irrational beliefs, or using it to decide what is the best course of events *against* an answer posed by rationality. For example, my theory would argue against a political party who were using emotional tactics to elicit reactions against an event or occurrence which was not immoral. This undoubtedly occurs often in countries where religion still holds a prime place in government, like in the USA, and can be demonstrated with reference to the commonplace, irrational arguments against gay marriage, amongst others. The fact that rationality doesn't motivate people currently is not a good criticism of my theory; indeed the probability that this theory may well turn out to be controversial would be down to the fact that rationality is currently devalued in society. The importance of the ideas that have compelled me to write rational morality implicitly note that rationality is not currently a good widespread motivator, and the reason that I am writing this is largely to argue that it should become one ahead of religious and basic emotional appeal, which happens in US political arguments on moral matters, for example. The likes of republican positions against gay marriage are actually prime candidates for exemplifying this kind of problem: we are told that gay marriage 'devalues' traditional marriage, or that it is 'unnatural', or even worse that it is against 'God's will'. These are not good arguments, but the emotional pull of terms like 'natural' or 'God's will' and the threatening sentiment of gay marriage 'devaluing' one's own are tailored made to be threatening to US culture. They do not actually make a great deal of sense, but primarily consist of emotional puppetry.

We should look at how exactly we do use emotion in every area though, not just in politics. Well known particle physicist Brian Cox is famed for believing that we need to open science to the masses: 'If we can persuade enough people that science is as wonderful as it is useful, then we will be far better equipped as a civilization to face the great challenges of the 21st century.'[40] He isn't wrong, and indeed my theory nods in agreement with Cox's beliefs on the subject. Many would take his principle further, to mean that we need to use emotive language and relate science to people in the real world, outside of academia. This, too, is absolutely necessary. However, with an area of science like rational morality, this gets messy, as it allows people to bring in emotion rather than rationality. Again, like the examples of politics in the USA: you can have one political party arguing for gay marriage, one arguing against it, and all kinds of emotional ploys on both sides with no reliance on facts or truths. The development of morality as a science, and of a scientific community dedicated to developing facts and ideas related to morality, would be of great benefit to reducing this irrational way of ruling societies. Like how we should be turning to evidence when we discuss science, we should do the same with morality.

---

[40] http://blogs.wsj.com/speakeasy/2012/02/20/why-quantum-theory-is-so-misunderstood/

Emotion isn't necessarily a worry, though. We find it easy, for example, to differentiate between scientific fact and the emotive language we might use to describe scientific facts. For instance stars don't really 'give birth' to things, and no one appears to be under the illusion that this means certain objects are children of the stars in any meaningful manner. No one is suing celestial objects for alimony, for example. But with morality we are dealing with how we should act, not how things do act. As a result, we are bound to be faced by new problems and one of these may well be the mixing of emotive, advocacy language, with moral facts. This is an area to be mindful of. At current, we especially need to be wary that it's likely the language of morality, and its inability to describe things rationally, which puts people off moral ideas as an objective, science based subject. People view emotion as personal and subjective (which it is) so if we speak in emotional terms about morality, it might have immediate effect of garnering donations for certain causes, but it isn't likely to foster a long term understanding of morality as being objective.

RATIONALITY IS A PATRIARCHAL CONCEPT

Postmodern descriptions of feminism often argue against ideas like rationality, as it is said to be a concept of male importance, forced by patriarchal hands[41]. Despite the blatantly irrational sexism of assuming that women are not as naturally rational as men (nothing could be further from the truth, as the capacity and tendency to be rational is equal in both sexes), it is that same paradoxical argument that was encountered earlier, the one that goes: "Why assume rationality as a base value?", whilst systematically assuming rationality as its base value, and being unable to assume otherwise.

---

[41] This is a general point of contention among this area of feminism in society. Individual feminists who argue similar points include: Lloyd, G, The Man of Reason: "Male" and "Female" in Western Philosophy (1984)

One can argue against a notion that says 'we ought to speak English' with an argument in English, because other equally valid languages exist and more languages can even be formulated which hold the same level of meaning as English does. One cannot argue against the importance of rationality whilst using rationality, though, precisely because there is no other option of formulating an alternative for truth finding[42]. This may be rational philosophy that has been largely hidden in this area up until now, but it makes a mockery of attempts to devalue rationality. Rationality is so necessary that it doesn't even make sense to assume it is not a base value. Not just in morality, but in everything. And a premise that purports we ought to be rational is assuming the very least that we must assume and no more. Remember that stating we need rationality for truth finding is no different to stating that we need to find truth to be truth finding.

This postmodern criticism itself is one that misunderstands the rationale behind appropriating rationality a place of value. It is assumed that because a woman's classic role in society is one of emotional strength, it is therefore the opposite of rationality. This is just not true. Classically speaking, a less scientific idea of rationality might believe it to be the opposite of emotion, but that doesn't hold true with what we know about rationality now. Emotions are intensely rational reactions that occur in relation to events in the real world. Responding with disgust to something you find

---

[42] Many times I have seen the solution of alternative forms of truth finding touted as being that of adding emotion into the process (for example Bryan Luke in 'Taming Ourselves or Going Feral? Toward a Nonpatriarchal Metaethic of Animal Liberation'). It's not clear how one could even create such a process which valued both rationality and emotion, without basically subjecting the rational system to all kinds of bias, yet this kind of post-modern argument doesn't seem overly concerned about its lack of rational consistency. In a bygone era, ideas which used rationality to criticise rationality might fall down as soon as analysis shows it to be irrational, yet post-modern studies seem to thrive simply by denouncing rationality as somehow prejudice (more claims which are questionable and currently evidence-less). Unsurprisingly, scientists have begun to speak up against this kind of non-sensical post-modernism, the first I was aware of being Paul Gross and Norman Levitt's wonderful but now dated 'Higher Superstition: The Academic Left and it's Quarrels With Science' in 1994/98.

disgusting is no less rational than responding with no specific reaction to something you have no conscious interest in. This criticism is based on prejudices from a bygone era and has no claim to be taken seriously.

There is undoubtedly truth to the claim that sexism is a problem in society and it's through this that we see where the post-modern feminist criticism has taken a wrong turn. Society still seems to deem women as less important than men, studies still find women to make less money than men for performing the same roles, and women are primarily portrayed as sexual or domestic objects/goddesses in advertisements while men are reduced to nowhere near the same level of objectification. There is also little doubt that this social problem of sexism causes an issue for a good many areas of science, as scientific institutions are still open to indulging sexism given that they are run by people who live in what still appears to be a sexist society. But this kind of analysis, which agrees with feminist theory on the level of social prejudice, does not amount to a criticism of rationality or scientific method. Indeed, if we subject morality to the same rigours of reason as other forms of science, like I have argued that we should, then sexism is impossible to justify due to it being a prejudice as blatantly immoral as racism. Allowing this permission for rationality to penetrate morality would fight that very same patriarchal led sexism that feminists must abhor. Far from being patriarchal, a fair analysis shows rationality to oppose prejudice, and formulates the very argument that feminists need to be using in order to grab progress. Opposing rationality in morality is paradoxical and incredibly self-defeating for any feminist.

IT IS RATIONAL TO BE SELFISH, NOT MORAL

I have already briefly argued against this idea in the previous chapter, but it is of significance for several reasons. The first point to note is that altruism is also rational. 'Survival of the fittest' in the 'most selfish wins' type was understood, for a long time, to be the rational view of how things are, and this very much informs this criticism of rational morality. However with what we now know about evolution, and about the nature of society, it is simply untrue to say that pure selfishness is an intelligent phenomenon; we know that it isn't, at least among humans. There may be incidences in which one is forced to practice self-defence, for example, and thus be 'selfish' in order to protect oneself. But this is not a general rule about society, and indeed it doesn't make sense to say that selfishness is the ideal rational state when working in mutually fulfilling collectives. To posit this is to misunderstand rationality past the shallowest level. If we are to accept morality as useful and truth-based, like a science, we must make it rational. That's a simple claim which, as previously discussed, proves itself.

Spiritual roots

Writing this book was not the first time I let on to my ideas about rational morality and indeed I have come across many spiritually minded moral advocates in the time before and during the writing. All seem to see rationality as somehow separate from ideas like kindness and compassion, as if they are simply not compatible. I have so far attempted to show that this is not the case (kindness and compassion spring from rational thinking, they are far from segregated), but this occurrence shows us a great deal about the roots of spiritual ideas.

Undoubtedly many people, if not all, are instilled with moral intuitions. As we have seen, we are products of a rich evolutionary history indeed, and tools like altruism have caused these intuitions because they are of great value. We intuitively needed to act morally in the past in order to survive in society. It is the media portrayal of the rational as somehow 'cold' or 'calculating' that is likely a big factor behind people's dismissal of rationality from being of moral use. The idea that rationality doesn't respect personal intuitions, and so is immoral, has in turn caused this. Rationality is seen to be critical of baseless religion and personal spiritual beliefs, so given the implication up to now that these things are markers of moral concepts like wellbeing, kindness and compassion, whilst rationality is seen to be a marker of cold calculation, it goes hand in hand that a desire to be moral and do what's right is tied up in inclinations for the spiritual and the religious rather than the rational.

We need look no further than the media for examples of the problem. Pushing the norms of society, the media posits characters like Dr. House from hugely successful TV serial *House M.D.*, or Counter Terrorist Agent Jack Bauer from the equally famous *24*, in order to tell us what rational people are like. These guys famously tend away from close relationships, make cutthroat decisions and go off the rails in their personal lives. A fair assessment would note that House and Bauer are rationally minded when it comes to their jobs, or gaining results in single minded missions, but fairly irrational and incompetent with the way they treat other people, or with situations which are more complex than to involve immediate results. It makes for excellent TV, undoubtedly, but not such a great advert for rationality. These are society's rational role models and no one would want to champion rationality based on their often disastrous lives and relationships.

This leads to some interesting conclusions, though. Spiritual beliefs may be delusions, but they exist because of (not in spite of) the desire to be rational. There is an evolutionary and culturally inbuilt sense that morality is important, and the desire to be spiritual comes from the desire to recognise this as well as scientific rationality (which we are also inbuilt to respect). These two things thus seem very separate until it is pointed out in clear, certain terms that morality *is* rational. Once we do this we can see spirituality in a fresh new light; not as some form of random irrational tendency, but rather as desperation to understand the world, and a desire not to be pigeonholed by a scientific method of looking at the world which is marketed as being cold and neutral on the subject of morality. Morality, which on a very basic level appears to be incompatible with our rational inclinations, is hardwired into us because it is so rationally useful. We thus strive to reject rationality as a moral cause because the evidence we think we are aware of (primarily evidence in the media, or else in philosophy books) shows us that rationality is incompetent at judging morality

Not only does this help to explain spirituality as a rational matter, it also provides an easy way for people with spiritual beliefs to see what is right. Spirituality is not necessary and needs not be invented or promoted any longer. We delude ourselves because of our natural desire to be both rational and altruistic (the latter being a form of rationality which we are told isn't rational, and so we invent spiritual ideas to, in a sense, oppose rationality), but we no longer need spiritual 'experiential truth' in order to make morality valuable. Once we can show morality to be an important scientific discipline, the need for spiritual explanations, like the need for religion, can gradually fade away. Just as non-morality based spiritual experiences can be rationally explained. The ability to see these spiritual experiences and morality both as rationally caused traits, makes them no less wonderful to behold. We can experience the complexity of our rational abilities, and even understand those of vampire bats or other animals, whilst wondering at how an amazingly adept process such as evolution could have instilled them within us. Every part of this is inspiring. In fact wondering at the complexity of reality in this way seems much more satisfying than wondering at the perceived randomness/arbitrary unknowability that spiritual explanations offered.

The roots of prejudice

This leads us on to one of the great uses of rational morality. In clearing the need for spirituality we can outwardly remove it as a necessity of any kind and thus show up the problems with it: the main one being that spirituality is born out of faith, which in turn is another word for prejudice.

As I feel necessary to explain throughout the book, I will do so again: this is not an insult to any person of faith, but rather it is an insult to the concept of faith, and a plea for people who currently hold belief and value in faith to see the moral problems with it. I'm not referring only to those who believe in a formally recognised faith (like that of organised religion), but also those who claim to have personal experience of a God that simply cannot be proved. Human beings are not rational machines, we find it easy to delude ourselves into comforting beliefs. In fact, we can explain our tendency to do this back to our evolutionary history, also[43].

The reason to forgo faith, and its corresponding religious and spiritual beliefs, is thus not just a result of direct rationality (though of course that's one reason, as it's certainly irrational and *we ought to be rational*) but also as a matter of moral motivation whether you agree with my theory or not. A society that values faith implicitly values beliefs that are formed with no evidence, and ergo promotes the idea that this is a positive or acceptable way to form beliefs. Anyone who disagrees with prejudice like racism, sexism or homophobia, must understand the structural problem with prejudice straight away, as it is formed in exactly the same way as a faith and values a method of forming beliefs that doesn't require rationality or proof. Faith works in *exactly* the same way as prejudice, and whilst faith isn't always going to (and might not often, even) result in prejudice, a society which values, defends and promotes faith based thinking is implicitly going to do the same to prejudice. Both are formed without need for evidence or rationality and, as a result, both will flourish in a society in which either is rampant. If you consider religion to be a sunflower growing in the organic compost of faith, then you had better be ready for the weeds of prejudice as well.

One can disagree with this to a degree (i.e., show religious people often value forms of anti-prejudice, or show other

---

[43] See: *Why We Believe in God(s). A Concise Guide to the Science of Faith. J. Anderson Thomson Jr, MD, with Clare Aukofer.*

causes of discrimination that don't breed faith), but as a structural matter the two are inseparable, so we can assert that as a general matter both will flourish in the same conditions. There is no better example than my favourite one, of American politics (sorry to any American's reading this: I am not purposefully discriminating, yours is simply a well-known situation). Only a country which values religion can have arguments in which one side believes the marriages of other people (homosexuals) will destroy their own (religious republicans), and further still believe them regardless of there being no evidence to back it up. There is absolutely no logic to this; it's a classic form of people believing anything you tell them because you both want the same thing. In this case the tradition of marriage to be purely between straight people. The onus is on us to begin making the connection between faith and prejudice as a practical matter, perhaps even before we start looking at engaging rational morality. We've no need to value faith as a way to be moral anymore, so there's no need to take the risk. Most problems of prejudice in society will appear completely unrelated to religion or spirituality, and as a direct causation they certainly are. Yet they both breed from a valuing of faith, and it's difficult to argue against this given that we know exactly similar events will almost certainly occur in exactly similar circumstances. Again, we are talking of basic logic.

SCIENTISTS ARE RATIONAL, BUT THEY ARE OFTEN NOT MORAL

So, it is claimed, if science is about being rational, and scientists are not particularly moral, why should we believe morality is rational? In many ways one assumes this criticism comes from the exact understanding people see on TV: again, Dr. House is a marvellous scientific mind on medicine, but is a *douchebag* in his social life and to his colleagues. Thus rational people are known to be cold and immoral, and the circle completes as people who study science feel compelled to be cold and neutral about morality (as it is the way their role models behave), whereas people who study morality become suspicious of science. Before we even begin, we must note this: it is the case that currently many scientists do not submit to my theory. Many, if not most scientists still believe that science is mute on the subject of morality and, as a result, it's commonplace to see incidences of scientists also being religious or spiritual. Similarly we see other scientists being neutral and relativist about it. This is to be expected and is by no means a criticism of rational morality, which would disagree with both of these positions, instead favouring a third, more rational way for scientists to look at morality. We can't expect scientists (who are members of society) to act rationally on the subject of morality when we keep teaching the whole of society (including the scientists) that morality is an intensely non-rational or irrational occurrence.

Rationality doesn't 'make' scientists act rationally

This slightly different criticism is certainly compelling at first glance. Yet first of all, we can question whether all current science is even rational in the first place. The ideal of science certainly is rationality, but much investigation that falls under the label of science at current might not even pass any tests of rationality. Science is primarily about testing hypotheses (guesses or beliefs that the scientist holds). And it might also be the case that some areas of science are more rooted in tradition than scientific reasoning. There might be a lot of 'Bad Science', so to speak, and indeed authors like Ben Goldacre[44] have made a career out of trying to dig these unscientific ideas out from under the umbrella of science.

But also, just because one's job is labelled as "a scientist", does not mean that one is necessarily rational in any other area of his/her life. Just as we know that many priests are not necessarily men of faith[45], many scientists are not necessarily men of reason. Indeed, there is less call for scientists to be

---

[44] http://www.badscience.net/about-dr-ben-goldacre/
[45] As Daniel Dennet explained in his Christmas Essay for the New Statesman magazine 2011 entitled "The Social Cell" p 50-53. (19 Dec 11 – 1 January 12 edition)

completely rational than there is for priests to be completely religious, given that priesthood is a lifestyle choice on top of a job, whereas science is mostly seen only as a job. So we'd expect the relationship to be more biased in terms of scientists deviating from their supposed roles. And, as I've stated, there is currently no recognised scientific form of morality to speak of; we are taught that morality is either spiritual in some way, or is relativist. The entire point of this theory is to make this case, and encourage us all (especially scientists) to acknowledge morality as a science.

Anyhow, scientific engagement can certainly be a result of a society that is solely valuing rationality, but it is also a result of any society that wants progress in any area of industry or medicine, for example. So it doesn't make sense to judge the actions of scientists as the actions of the rational, as this would be the morality of current science and not the science of morality (the former being something that is entirely dependent on the society in which scientific investigation is taking place, and not necessarily a sign of what is rational). We cannot judge the ability of rationality to create consistent morality until we have a society, and scientific community, which values only rationality and is educated to accept that morality is an area of science like I am arguing in this theory. Until then, the scientists we see will be a reflection of the 'contain rationality to our jobs' types that society creates.

MANY WILL REFUSE TO BE RATIONAL

Essentially this moral theory suffers the same problem as any moral theory. Many people simply don't care and so will not begin valuing rational morality. This doesn't mean the theory is wrong, it simply means that what needs to be done to advance it has to be creative and intelligent in its approach. However I believe this theory stands a better chance than most, as a practical matter. It is less likely, in my mind, that people in increasingly secular societies will reject this theory than a fantastically created morality like religion or classical moral realism, for several reasons.

Valuing what is natural to us

Putting morality into its place as a rational matter is doing what is natural to us. Things like abstract moral facts are not particularly good motivators, and neither is a moral code passed down from an abstract concept like God, which many do not now believe in anyway. Abstract moral facts might relate to our intuitions (like science also relates to our intuitions) but our most basic workings are based around rationality (and these push science too, but not spiritual morality). Ergo, fantastical ideas like classic moral realism relate to people on some surface level, but they realistically distance people from morality by putting it out there as some unknowable source. As a result it has led to high levels of understanding morality as an entirely relativist concept; actions of moral intent seem to have become more of an ambiguous, personal matter or else of forced legal/social obligation, than something of real, solidly understood value.

Take conservation, for example. The World Wildlife Fund (WWF) is one of the world's largest charities, yet it is difficult to see exactly how rational it is. It aims to help endangered species, yet these species are becoming extinct in the modern world because, for whatever reason, they no longer have a place to thrive. The WWF is so successful at eliciting donations because it shows individual, magnificent looking animals in its adverts, and appeals both to our senses of awe and compassion, as well as to our sense of not wanting to lose things 'forever'. Such campaigns appeal to an uninformed sense of 'what if we need the Panda at a later time?! It will be gone!'

Criticism of such charities is met by fierce complaints from patrons, who mount the criticism as cold, rational and un-compassionate. They are right, but only because compassion and warmth instead of rationality would be counter-productive in this instance. Their response, though, is the equivalent of children's charities defending our will to ignore the masses at the expense of the one child.[46] The WWF does not

---

[46] Slovic, P. (2007).

save Pandas because it believes Pandas are sentient and it cares for their wellbeing. It cares for Pandas out of misplaced guilt that there is no longer a place for them in the world, or perhaps even out of misunderstanding the reason Pandas can no longer exist naturally (because we have destroyed their habitats, not because we need to gather them into Zoos, etc.). If the WWF were being rational, it would be every bit as concerned for pigs or cows who are sentient and die in their millions every day simply because we find frivolous, irrational reasons to disrespect their interests (mainly out of that same irrational 'survival of the fittest' belief that we are top of the food chain, so have no reason to be anything but cold and calculated in the direction of other species). Realistically, the WWF is not valuing the interests of sentient individuals — either in terms of saving individuals based on their sentience, or conserving the environment for these individuals to live in — but is valuing an abstract concept that has run away with its own success. The organisation has become so good at soliciting donations and functioning as a business that its economic interest in surviving as a company now outweighs its interests to look inward and realise it is largely doing nothing of moral value.

What the WWF (and its position in society as a respected charity) shows us is that even those moral causes we currently have in society are almost entirely borne out of ignorance, to the degree that we should question each and everyone one of them as to the point of their existence at all. If we are each respecting the interests of every other sentient individual in the first place, what is the point of most charity? And until we get to that stage, why shouldn't every charity be focused on simply creating a respect for sentience full stop, as a method to get there? The list of questions we need to ask is huge if we begin being rational about explicit moral movements like charities, and these are but two of them.

The idea of rational morality agrees with Harris in stating that morality is about the wellbeing of sentient individuals. And in doing so it not only has logic on its side, it also creates a morality of simplistic beauty with which we can reduce every one of these ambiguous causes into nothingness, and instead form an over-arching rational meaning which actually gives purpose to moral causes rather than individual pressure groups. We may still need some charities, sure, but a charity to appease every person's moral guilt so they themselves don't have to recognise the most important one's (those that respect the starving or the homeless, or the billions of farm animals) in favour of their personal aesthetic taste in *liking* tigers? That's irrational and it simply has to go; we're doing nothing but pummelling our rational abilities into a tiny box which we can hide away so we can follow our gut instincts. These are charities of a time when religious, personal spirituality ruled the earth and many of them likely no longer have a place under their current guises.

Similarly, with simplicity comes motivation. It's no wonder people are not currently motivated to be moral. Merge the fact that so many ambiguous charities and moral causes exist (our wide ranging charity scene reflects personal tastes, rather than the interests of the needy) with the fact that the current moral landscape is entirely inept at giving anyone a truthful reason to act morally in the first place, and we have an astoundingly hopeful reason to start throwing our support behind the rational form of morality like I advocate for in this book. This theory will not just be relevant to those with strong moral intuitions, it will also be of relevance to those who want to live in and understand reality, and I've yet to see a compelling reason how anyone, anywhere falls outside of this group. Even the religious and the spiritualist individuals are so because they believe they have rational reason to be. This theory, despite being heavily critical of such beliefs, should provide an excellent challenge in asking why they need to hold these beliefs anymore, and further in challenging any 'experiential truths' which they think are currently relevant. People are spiritual because it is functional for them to be so. This theory takes most of that remaining functionality away and clears the path for rational thinking and morality to merge properly.

4. A Science of Morality isn't About Numbers

Inherent, it seems, in all secular work on morality is the belief that it is about numbers to some degree. It's the idea that if morality is to be considered rational in some way then we will eventually be able to create formulae for deciding what is best to do in any given situation. Like in physics, measurements and understanding about any given issue will cause us to be able to look at it as sets of facts and numbers, and thus make our decisions based on formulae in some way.

Yet, as touched upon in the last chapter, human beings are not good judges of morality as a rational matter. At least not yet. We have evolved through a rich history, but by no means have we become perfect. It does seem initially intuitive to think that as we progress – as we become more educated about the reality we inhabit – we will be much better placed to make these sorts of decisions. In the same way as we are all much better placed on thinking about the best ways to keep our family warm with our better, modern understanding of the laws of insulation, perhaps one day we will all be better placed to make ethical decisions in our everyday life with a better understanding of morality. After all, none of us could recite laws of insulation, but we all grasp the idea in a way which could be said to be a summarising understanding (ie, that a blanket will help to keep us warmer than not having a blanket).

So that may be, but to think of morality as a formulaic numbers game is to miss the point. It is not sensible to assume that we will ever be well enough educated to make decisions like formulaic machines. A simple example should show why that is.

THE 'MEDICAL EMERGENCY' SIMILARITY

Consider medical emergencies. Over the eras our understanding of how the body works has increased dramatically. Even in as short a time period as two hundred years, we might look back in shock at the things doctors did in the name of improving our health, or solving our medical problems. Disease was common place, and not just down to bad safety rules (like those which are mistakenly blamed for causing the spread of MRSA in modern hospitals[47]), but due to the lack of understanding we had regarding how diseases were spread, or how the human body works.[48]

As ever expanding as our knowledge of medicine is, most of us now have a better grasp. This stretches far beyond the hospital and many of us (while not medical experts) would be able to provide basic first aid assistance. Similarly, we are much better able to avoid certain illnesses by knowing rules about health and safety, and about the basics of how disease spreads. But still, most of us would be ill-placed to perform heart surgery or a trachea bypass like surgeons or paramedics, respectively, could. Despite our growing societal understanding of internal medicine, this much has not changed and is not likely to change.

Indeed, it seems irrational to predict a time when all of us are educated to the degree in which we might be able to perform heart surgery. Furthermore, we don't consider this a problem, as we train people to fulfil that role in society. We should view morality in partly the same way, but with one notable exception – laws and rules should replace doctors and paramedics as the guides.

---

[47] The science journalist Ben Goldacre, referenced so often in this book, writes an excellent piece on this subject in Bad Science, where he uncovers the fact that no MRSA has ever been found living on dirty mops or in dusty corners of hospitals – it is a myth that MRSA comes from dirty hospitals, and an unfortunate myth that an ignorant media completely promotes.

[48] Famously, for a long time we considered smell to be the thing that carried disease. Whilst this was scientifically understood at the time (as bad smells often do naturally alert us to dangerous things to avoid) we progressed to a better understanding of germs and bacteria, and as a result we can avoid diseases better with our knowledge that it isn't the smell itself that is problematic.

I think this is a fair analogy. With our growing under-standing of medicine, each of us has become more informed and our perspectives of potential danger have changed from, say, trying to stay away from smells (which were once thought to carry disease) to trying to neutralise harmful germs (which are the true carriers of disease). The same should be true of morality, and as we come to know more about how morality works (in its rational role) so we should all be able to live our lives making more informed decisions. But as this improves, we should be comfortable knowing that we need moral rules, like we need heart surgeons. We are not all ever going to be well placed to calculate formulas in real time as to the best moral decisions to make, in the same way as we are not all ever going to be educated to perform heart surgery. The complexities of modern life and the complexities of medical emergencies are similar, in this respect.

FAILING TO PLAN IS PLANNING TO FAIL

I didn't think a saying of an old business studies teacher (which was shouted at me, through lesson after lesson, to explain the importance of business plans), would be cropping up in anything I'd write on the subject of rational morality, but it demonstrates the point perfectly: if we fail to plan for the kinds of individuals we are, then the kinds of individuals we are will ruin the best intentions we have. Or more succinctly, as one of my least favourite teachers would put it, failing to plan is planning to fail.

I use the example of euthanasia often to illustrate a point where it might be a lesser of two evils to outlaw someone's ability to help another person to die. And yet I understand, perfectly well, that if one person wants to die there should be no reason – whatsoever – why the state should be morally allowed to intervene and stop a friend, family member or even a perfect stranger from helping them to do it. Indeed, it seems highly symptomatic of a society in the twilight of the grasp of Abrahamic religious tradition that groups might oppose suicide as a personal choice at all.

However, if it can be shown that allowing a rule to disregard murder on grounds of euthanasia would allow for the murder of the elderly, or other dependant individuals – or in fact any individuals – against their will, then we need to strongly consider whether it is right to allow euthanasia.

As I previously stated, I am not an expert on the 'ins and outs' of this case, and my personal opinion is that allowing for euthanasia under certain circumstances would not be problematic. However, I use this example to show a point – moral rules and their subsequent legal jurisdiction are required because human beings are not perfect rational agents. Murder happens, personal greed can overcome the rational decision making process, etc., and facts like these have to be taken into account. Failing to plan for the imperfection of humans is, quite simply, planning to fail. It's nothing more than living in a fantasy world, casting away practical concerns in favour of holding onto theoretical ideas.

SHALLOW PRAGMATISM

The atheist ethicist and author Peter Singer takes a position of utilitarianism, believing that suffering and pleasure are what matters, and that due to this we must make our decisions based on what will maximise pleasure and minimise suffering.[49] I have a lot of respect for Singer – he and I share some opinions in the subject of animal ethics, and also share much more on the subject of the need for secular ethics. I, however, do not agree with his position as a utilitarian.

The flaws in utilitarianism are many and well known about. For instance, where do you draw the line, when something like gang rape seemingly proves a moral act by maximising pleasure among many and causing only one person to suffer? Among many utilitarians suffering is therefore regarded as a graver thing to avoid than pleasure is to be caused, which makes utilitarianism an essential grasping on one fact rather than two – that suffering is meaningful and must be alleviated.

---

[49] Practical Ethics, Singer, P. 2nd Edition, 1993.

Among other problems, this brings us back to the initial one of moral realism, which simply states there is a moral fact with little or no relevance to reality other than to our intuitions, or our behaviour – intuitions being that aspect of human beings most flawed as a method of deriving facts (especially in societies with such a heavily religious history, whereby all manner of intuitions naturally support what is scientifically absurd), and deriving a moral law from behaviour being yet another *ought* drawn from an *is*.

In this respect, whether choosing Singer's utilitarianism, or any form of rights based moral realism instead (like Tom Regan's for example[50]), we are simply doing the moral equivalent of choosing between Christianity and Islam. There's no evidence on either side, just a will to believe in one rather than the other – a decidedly irrational choice in the first place, held up only by posturing from all sides upon which is the right answer[51]. This is a conflict which has been common-place in religion for many years, and it should worry us as rationalists, since people debating made up ideas which are supported only by 'intuitions' or 'ought-is deductions' are unlikely to bear the fruit of truth.

Similarly utilitarianism falls foul of exactly the problem which I discussed above – failing to plan. To assert utilitarianism successfully, despite all of its problems, one still has to assert certain moral rules (like making murder illegal), so in essence why bother with utilitarianism at all? It speaks to those parts of us which like to formulate and judge issues, sure, but aren't there better theories that do this? The theory of rational morality which I am putting forth certainly speaks to our rational intuitions, as well as to our will to formulate ideas. It suffers none of the problems of utilitarianism, as it doesn't make any unjustified meta-physical claims about morality.

A reformed version of utilitarianism might accept that suffering is the thing we should be worried about, rather than putting so much value on pleasure. It might also agree with

---

50 The Case for Animal Rights. Regan. T. 1983.
51 Animal Rights and Human Obligations. Singer, P. and Regan, T. 1976.

the idea of rights and of laws against indecent immoral acts. However, it is always going to miss the point – it subscribes to what I would call 'shallow pragmatism'.

What rational morality asks us to do is think logically. We do not have evidence for deities setting rules, so let's ignore the idea of God-formed moral facts. We do not have evidence for independent moral facts at all, so let's ignore the idea of independent moral facts. We do, however, have evidence that morality is in some way rational, that we all seem to value morality, and therefore that we ought to be rational about it (in the most meaningful way in which we can speak of 'ought'), so let's discover what moral facts there are by using consistency and rationality. But utilitarianism, at its worst, asks us to think in a shallow pragmatic way (this is known as 'act utilitarianism') whereby we must judge each act on each act's merits, or worse, judge morality by suffering, alone. This is failing to plan and is symbolic of a theory which misunderstands our human nature of not being perfect, rational machines. Furthermore, it asserts a 'fact' that suffering is the marker of morality. Of course suffering is an important aspect of wellbeing, but boiling morality down to just this one principle makes no rational sense. We are back with the classic problems of moral realism when we hear such assumptions.

Earlier, I also considered the criticism: 'scientists aren't rational', which in a more fulfilling way might translate as 'people cannot be perfectly rational'. Whilst this isn't a problem for rational morality, it is a problem for act utilitarianism. Rule utilitarianism (which involves following the best rules in order for society to bring about the most good/least suffering) is slightly better than act utilitarianism (following the best decision to bring about the most good/least suffering in any single circumstance), in that it takes on board the nature of human beings as animals, rather than rational machines, yet it is still problematic. It holds at its centre the idea that when faced with a decision we must choose the best course of action based on the general rule that will create the most happiness. And yet, it still misses the point in a magnificent way: happiness doesn't sum up all that is to be considered about morality. There's no evidence that happiness could define morality better than wellbeing, and even if there were, we'd still be better placed deriving that evidence via rational morality rather than via a blatant assumption.

Again, reformed versions of this theory take on board suffering *and* happiness. But that's all it ever is. Life is boiled down to two extremes, avoiding suffering and provoking happiness – two moral facts that do not exist independently, and for which there is no reason to believe they do. The idea I have put forth is, essentially, that we all agree on a definition of morality and then extend it logically – this is always going to be a better bet.

It might be argued that once one accepts rational morality, and the non-existence of independent moral facts, then rule utilitarianism (as explained) is fair game. But why? Why on earth do we need to think about life in this manner? Harris rightly defines morality as being about the wellbeing of sentient individuals. Why do we need to make this about suffering and happiness, as two polar opposites – why not stick with the original definition of morality and make our rules based on the practical application of the wellbeing of sentient individuals in any given circumstance? We can still use ideas like minimising suffering and maximising pleasure, for instance, without reducing our entire theory and moral code to it (even if it turns out 99% of our moral code is to do with suffering and pleasure). A rational morality doesn't need to ever reduce to utilitarianism, unless in individual situations – in which case it isn't utilitarianism, it is a single equation or summing up based on similar factors to those which utilitarianism evokes wholesale.

It seems, indeed it has always seemed to me, that utilitarianism is fairly popular among ethicists because it plays to our intuitions about wanting to judge and formulate. It comes out best in exceptional thought experiments where we are posed the question that shows we would always do that which caused the least suffering or that which causes the most happiness. Yet it misses the point that the only moral concern should be wellbeing, and that suffering and happiness are aspects of this rather than the other way around. We live in a world where the wellbeing of sentient individuals (both humans and other animals) is routinely ignored and where people seem to be happiest when choosing what the value of their own lives should be (without being told, from some meagre assessment, that it is 'suffering' to be avoided and 'pleasure' to be caused – and indeed without being forced to live by rules that establish this order). Indeed the two emotions (suffering and pleasure) interact on such a spectrum that they can often form in situations in which one directly causes the other[52]. Formulae that aim to be so precise in setting rules do not make sense given what we know about the mental states which it is aiming to either reduce or provoke, and only appear to make sense if we are to go back to the fantastical notion of 'independent moral facts' that state 'suffering should be avoided' – facts which can be shown not to exist.

'Wellbeing', albeit a difficult to define concept itself, is as Harris states no different to valuing 'health', which is a similarly hard to define concept. We don't need to reduce health to being about pain and pleasure, so there's no need to do so with ethics – not when wellbeing already does the job quite nicely. We can in fact amend what wellbeing involves if required, as science investigates further.

As a result, it makes sense to call the corresponding theory which looks at more than two precise mental states, and more than individual decisions in individual circumstances, as one

---

[52] This is very much a philosophical point, but one which is built into our understanding of emotion. Imagine being given an ice cream right now. Taste good? Now imagine being starved and kept from water for 3 days, then being given an ice cream. Taste even better? Of course it does. We are evolutionarily wired to get more pleasure from something we desperately need, than something we just want. Whilst it is ethically questionable to frustrate needs in order to cause greater pleasure, this kind of example does demonstrate that the two extremes of suffering and pleasure are not as unconnected as people think. They likely do not exist as two separate emotions, like we imagine, but rather as mental states which have an effect on one another.

of 'thorough pragmatism' – a form of pragmatism like physics, which is based in rationality and so 'provable' at its very beginnings, without having to become shallow in its application of valuing unknowable consequences. It is perhaps no surprise that a solid form of 'thorough pragmatism' is one and the same as a scientific rational morality.

THE RATIONALIST'S DISTRACTION – NON-HUMAN ANIMALS

Although heavily referenced in the work of Singer and an increasing number of secularist thinkers, rationalists appear to be heavily distracted from talking about non-human animals. In the rare instances where they are discussed, prejudice and faith based thinking call the shots. Perhaps this comes from the long traditions which the western world has had in believing animals do not have souls, or it could be because of the rich, rights based tradition which has seen animals denigrated to the status of unable participants in a contractual agreement to respect each other's rights. Who knows? The fact is that such views of morality are no longer relevant and animals are now on the moral agenda.

The better angels of our nature

Steven Pinker's recent analysis of the historical decrease in violence[53], leading to our being able to confidently state that we now live in a more peaceful world than ever before, is wonderful in showing something this book is indebted to. That is the idea that as we tend toward and become more rational (or as Pinker puts it, as we 'extend reason'), we also become more peaceful and civilised. I believe Pinker is mistaken in one respect, in that he believes one of the major causes is how empathy has been rationally extended, whereas I believe empathy itself is a symptom of rationality. We've no need to attribute the cause of a more peaceful world to empathy, so much as to increasing rationality (whereby

---

[53] The Better Angels of Our Nature. Pinker, S. 2011.

empathy is a natural part), but this isn't a philosophical book review of Pinker's otherwise excellent analysis, so I will leave that discussion for another time. My views on rationality will be very clear by now, in any event.

Pinker's analysis of violence focuses less on animals than humans, though, despite the history of humanity imparting more violence on other animals (which still sits at an astounding 1 trillion animals a year, as a conservative estimate[54]) than other humans. Indeed, in just a single year one could be confident in the claim that we commit more violence against other animals than we ever have against human beings. The numbers are huge. The focus on humans shows something important – we like to add animals into moral equations as a rational matter, praising ourselves for our ability to remove our religious forefathers' irrational ideas, but we don't like to treat them to the levels of equality which, rationally speaking, their traits deserve. Perhaps a problem of our own 'shallow pragmatic' making.

Indeed, despite the almost complete opposition that this theory has to Peter Singer's work, it might be claimed that he is the only well-known rationalist to academically admit the equality of other animals in issues like suffering, stating as he does that, "All the arguments to prove man's superiority cannot shatter this hard fact: in suffering the animals are our equals."[55]

Pinker's mistake in this (which is forgivable as an academic matter given the focus on human history in education, though perhaps not forgivable as an ethical matter) may not disprove his theory, as it might still turn out that despite our horrendous, continuing exploitation of other animals, it is no worse than it used to be. So when adding to this calculation

---

[54] http://fishcount.org.uk/fish-welfare-in-commercial-fishing/estimate-of-fish-numbers. The number of aquatic animals killed alone is said to be in the trillions, however this figure is truly unknowable as these animals are measured in tons rather than individual lives. Around 60 billion land animals are said to be killed each year but, again, this figure moves around and is truly unknowable. What we do know for sure is that these figures are unimaginably high.
[55] Animal Liberation. Singer, P. 1975.

the 'better' state of inter-human violence, then we may well have definitely been in progress toward peace. However, it shows that we are wholly distracted when it comes to other animals – the one big, hidden prejudice of our time is most definitely 'speciesism'. And given our human penchant for the irrational (do you know anyone who doesn't indulge religion, spirituality or moral realism in some form?!), it is ironic that we largely excuse our exploitation of sentient individuals in other species with the excuse that *they* aren't rational.

THE UTILITARIAN MISTAKE –
WELFARISM AS A MARKER OF 'BETTERNESS'

Pinker's comments on animals are backed up by beliefs in 'welfarism'. This constitutes the animal welfare laws that have cropped up in modern society, as well as facts like how we no longer burn cats or regularly exploit animals in frivolous forms of entertainment. So he believes that, all other things being equal, this kind of analysis constitutes an improvement for non-humans. But, this belief is a common mistake.

It seems rational morality disagrees with everyone it mentions, on at least one point[56] - such is the process when delving into largely unvisited subject areas - and there is another author following this line to be considered, who has considerable evidence to add to this subject. Evidence which shows Pinker and Singer to be incorrect in their assumptions about welfare reform, from which Singer has made a career by championing and which Pinker uses to erroneously back up his theory that things are now better for animals.

Legal scholar and animal rights theorist Gary L. Francione has been making the case against welfare reform, on moral and practical grounds, since the early 90's. We can reject his theory of 'animal rights' itself on the basis of its insistence, like most others, on using classical moral realism. Indeed Francione has made it clear in various places that he doesn't

---

[56] Which one might state is an advantage, given the theory draws from the work of several academics and creates new light with several bases.

agree rationality is any sort of guarantor of morality, and believes science has nothing to say about morality. Similarly, it must be noted that his insistence on animals having just the one right, not to be used as property, is based on the idea that it is simply an independent moral fact that we must not exploit other animals (or sometimes he quotes the moral fact of non-violence). I reject this on the grounds that it is irrational, classical moral realism, much like Singer's. Francione forms the Islam to Singer's Christianity, as the analogy would go, and as such, Francione's consistent criticism of Singer seems decidedly religious in nature.

However, Francione's work on the practical side of welfare reform is of immense importance. In *Animals, Property and The Law*[57], Francione makes several breakthroughs in his legal examination of welfare reform. He notes, firstly, that animals are legally seen as property, and any attempt to improve the welfare of property has to be done by summing up the effect on current persons – i.e., human beings. Attempts to improve animal welfare (take the PETA gained partial success in getting chain restaurants to slaughter chickens in more humane ways[58]) have to be done by making it seem more economically efficient. As a result, not only do the animal groups, like PETA who are pushing for the changes, have to find success through earmarking economic improvements for companies in producing the animal products, they also can only be successful in getting improvements which do not cost more than the improvement is economically bringing in. As a result, though theoretically possible to improve animal welfare this way, welfarism as an idea is incredibly limited in affording protection to animals. The real way to improve their conditions is to grant them a legal status akin to persons, rather than property, and we simply can't do this while we societally see them as products to be utilised for our consumption.

I will further discuss the practical limits of welfarism later in the book, however, this idea is almost entirely missed in

---

[57] Animals, Property and the Law. Francione, G. L. 1995.
[58] http://www.peta.org/features/the-case-for-controlled-atmosphere-killing.aspx

Singer's and in Pinker's work. There is an assumption that these welfare regulations are 'better' for animals, but the truth is that there is little evidence for this. Indeed, from Francione's work we *know* that the individual welfare regulation that groups like PETA pick isn't due to its ability to significantly improve the lives of animals, but more down to the case PETA can make for industry taking the change on board – the regulation is picked solely because of its economic efficiency and thus potential for success (sometimes referred to as 'picking the low hanging fruit'). Yet as far as PETA are concerned, with their policy of 'animals are not ours to use', improving a company's ability to use animals efficiently is neither a smart move nor a rational one.

Add to this the fact that all of these large, successful animal groups are essentially businesses, in which their survival to 'fight for the animals' depends on their ability to create success by picking economically efficient welfare regulations, thus garnering donations for continued activity through such public success, and it becomes apparent that welfare regulation is not as 'for the animals' as it seems. Individuals creating the campaigns are employed by the groups for their ability to create successes, and successes themselves are manufactured through economically efficient arguments – it becomes difficult to see at what point the regulation campaigns are being judged by their ability to improve things for animals at all, as the volunteers (who do pretty much what the business executives say) are the only ones appearing to value the animals' interests, and they are not the ones who create the policies. There appears to be an unbreakable, ineffective circle in progress.

Furthermore, all welfarism rests on the philosophical assumption that animals simply *are* helped by welfare regulation, on a conceptual scale of betterness which no-one seems to have bothered to create. Given Francione's mountain of legal examination, the lack of holding animal groups to such a scale, when we know charities are erring into irrationality (as earlier discussed regarding the WWF) is suspect. So more work obviously needs to be done in the area if Pinker's claim is to hold any water. But let's also think about non-human animal interests a little.

I spent many years growing up on an egg farm. We had one big shed with, from what I remember, around ¾ 'free range hens' and ¼ 'barn hens'. The difference between the two labels in terms of consumer confidence is huge, and indeed advocates like Singer see legislation regarding free range eggs as some of the most significant improvements for animals, ever[59]. Yet as a young teenager growing up on a hen farm with both free range and non-free range, I hope I can be forgiven for stating that for non-human animals the differences are miniscule at best. "One big cage" is really the only way to look at free range, as opposed to a smaller one or lots of little ones for non-free range. The 'betterness' is very definitely in the heads of humans and marketing executives, and also unexplainably in the work of some rationalist ethicists.

The reason for this difference between industrial reality and consumer perception is that welfarism, as well as relying on rationally unsound utilitarianism (PETA's 'animal rights philosophy' is actually the 'animal welfare' philosophy championed by Singer, if you examine it), rests on very human concepts. One will often hear an advocate for free range or 'humane' alternatives to regular animal products saying things like 'If I was a farmed chicken, I'd be grateful for the extra room'. But a chicken can't have these thoughts, not in any way similar to that which is being expressed. A chicken, to our knowledge, does not form mental coping mechanisms based on the assumption that 'it could be worse'. Indeed, don't we think this is a uniquely human characteristic, based on some fairly advanced forms of rational thinking – or at least shouldn't we, until proven otherwise? So why are we making the argument as if a

---

[59] A point Francione references and takes Singer to task on here. Singer's ideas appear philosophically sound, but it is the legal detail and practical theory that brings him crashing down to Earth.
http://www.abolitionistapproach.com/replacing-one-cage-with-another/

chicken would think in this way? Welfarism, despite its speciesist results, is built on decidedly anthropomorphic and unscientific assumptions. On the one hand, champions of welfarism criticise more 'extreme' forms of 'animal rights' (like veganism) for anthropomorphism, and yet use the same reasoning in justifying their own beliefs.

What should be obvious about any mammals, and even certain groups of mentally impaired humans, is that they do not necessarily form coping mechanisms. They may get used to suffering, but this doesn't mean they will suffer any less as time goes on. Even if they do form coping mechanisms, as far as we know they do not have the conceptual ability to theorise in a way such as 'Well, it's bad in here but at least I'm not in this exact spot, but in a smaller cage, or closer to the other hens in this already small shed'. So why do we assume that by removing the cage, but replacing it with a bigger cage, or a huge cage (shed) just crammed with lots more birds (maybe increasing the space allowed the chicken by an inch, or even ten inches) it would be better? One thing animals share with humans is a rich variety of interests, and slightly increasing one of them in this way will likely have no psychological benefits for a rationally less capable individual like a chicken. It screams to our human will to formulate and adjudge 'betterness', as does utilitarianism as a whole, but it appears to do little if anything for the non-human animal.

We must also take on board the stark fact–which we are also indebted to Francione for–that the animals currently in sheds will never experience the higher welfare regulation themselves. Animals on farms live from maybe a few months to 5 years[60], whereas welfare regulation takes many more years than this to come into force (due to the earlier mentioned legal and economic problems – governments must give businesses time to implement changes as animals are not persons, they are

---

[60] http://www.baahaus.org/faqs.html Shows the life spans as follows: Beef Cattle 10-18 months, Chickens 6-8 weeks, Dairy Cows around 4 years, Lambs 3-5 months, Pigs 6-7 months, Turkeys 4-5 months. These figures are best guesses really, and we can confidently assert that animals live anywhere up to around 4/5 years as an economic matter.

products). So we are not improving the lives of animals now; we are simply making the lives of animals in the future less horrible for us to look at. No animal will be thinking "Phew! I'm glad I wasn't born 10 years ago", just as no animals will be thinking "This is bad, but it could be worse", as far as we know. And yet welfarism requires this to be true.

Suffering of the sort experienced on any farm, where any animal is used as a piece of economic property, or in any slaughterhouse where animals are killed, is of a significant level. This is evolutionary common sense – unless the cows are being sat in padded stalls, being fed their favourite foods, surrounded by families and all killed in their sleep by pills ground up in their food, then of course death is a major panic for a sentient, conscious organism. We're sentient in order to avoid death more efficiently, so it makes a lot of sense that we'd suffer greatly from not being able to avoid it. Arguably that's the only reason suffering exists. In any case, it takes a huge level of irrational ignorance to pretend the animals are being killed painlessly, or to believe that welfare regulation is significantly better. 'Padding the water board', as Francione analogises[61], will not make a difference to the animals whose suffering will still be significant, as well as the most horrendous experience of their short lives. An extra ten inches here, or a couple of trips outside, does nothing to alleviate 90% of the suffering an animal experiences – so we should be forgiven for asking if an animal who has never experienced worse would really be experiencing a better life of any sort in the new welfare 'enriched' conditions, let alone one worth campaigning for.

If we add these irrational conceptual mistakes that welfare regulation makes in its philosophising, to the fact that we now kill more non-human animals than ever before (consider industrial fishing especially, which dwarfs the 60 billion land animals killed yearly with an unconceivable figure of at least a trillion, as mentioned earlier), then it becomes clear that

---

[61] Quoted from http://www.thescavenger.net/animals/the-abolitionist-approach-to-animal-rights-145.html

although we are arguably progressing in levels of civility and peace thanks to reason, violence isn't decreasing as we are finding ways to alleviate our consciences with more violence than ever before toward nonhuman individuals. Simply put, welfarism makes us feel better about violence toward animals – it is nothing but faith-based, misplaced compassion.

It was Edward Augustus Freeman who supposedly noted that, "The awful wrongs and sufferings forced upon the innocent, helpless, faithful animal race, form the blackest chapter in the whole world's history."[62] Technological advances now allow us to exploit animals with less appreciative qualities, not just the helpless faithful ones, but he still has a point. Animals, it seems, are the last moral taboo and given the scarcity of rationalists who accept this, it is vital that they be considered heavily in any practical applications of rational morality.

---

[62] Freeman was a historian famed for his writing on the Norman Conquest; however appeared to write little, to my knowledge, on animals. I include this quote with a note that it was supposedly stated by him, but as with so many historical quotes one can't be sure. It's better than not knowing who it was by and so just attributing it to Mark Twain on the basis that it sounded clever, which everyone else seems to do.

5. Practical Ethics

PRELUDE

In one sense, rational morality can appeal to a variety of current moral and social movements in backing up claims made on behalf of rights-bearers, or in opposing unfair, irrational systems that are impacting on a group of individual's well-being. The main difference rational morality puts forth is that we have to change the way we think about morality, with practical application being something of an objective, fact based nature, not a subjective, personal taste or a spiritually posited one. There are right and wrong answers to be gleaned, and many of these answers will undoubtedly already have social movements pushing them due to the rich variety of moral beliefs currently existing in the world. Similarly, many current moral movements do not make the slightest bit of sense as a moral matter (for example, the work of conservationists to capture animals, display them in zoos and force them to breed, as a way of helping the biological category of species rather than the sentient individuals who may suffer as a result of such action).

With this in mind, I was wary about whether this section was a good idea at all, upon first planning the book. People often judge the value of ideas in relation to how well the idea sits with what they believe. So upon pointing out the practical application of rational morality, it is easy to worry that some may discard the theory altogether simply by disagreeing with what it may require them to do. Given the wide range of moral ideas currently in human cultures across the world, this is undoubtedly a worry which will surface with some reactions. And hence at this point, I urge self-critical honesty and perspective while reading the next few chapters; think of the effect on others' entire lives, rather than the few minutes, hours or even days it may take of yours. The great scientific advancements of our time were not made by people sitting on their couches for eight hours a day, but were painstakingly rooted out in labs or in the field. These advancements themselves were made possible by pioneers of another time who were routinely oppressed by religious authorities that did not want truth to oppose the comfortable myths that had been created. Being morally and rationally consistent will not require this level of effort, but undoubtedly will require you do something — so such a change in perspective is appreciated.

These initial worries I had were quickly dissolved, as practical application is what rational morality is all about. The point of it is to show that we currently think erroneously about morality. As a result, with classical forms of moral theory we see people talking in abstracts, and considering the most basic of ideas as constitutive of 'facts', or even supporting charities based on intuitive appeal to erroneous moral norms and values. However with rational morality there is a real form of specific consequentialism. Rational morality is a realistic way to think about morality, built from science and rational consistency, and as such it doesn't take the view that morality is subjective and to be applied as to one's personal opinions, or one's knee jerk reactions. Sure there will be areas where we can't honestly know what is best to do, as always. However, right now there is still an awful lot about which there is moral confusion, spreading from a growing misperception about moral relativism, which itself is most probably a misplaced extension of liberalism with regards to respecting one another (in the sense that one can't claim that moral facts are real, so one must respect all opinions about it equally). As stated throughout, rational morality shows this idea to be intellectually bankrupt, that there are many factual statements and actions we can make about reality, and that moral relativism itself makes claims about morality which aren't true.

To my mind, there are at least five main areas in society where morality is confused in the aforementioned way; on some of which opinion is currently entirely turned in the wrong direction. There lies the commercial danger in asserting a new theory in a practicable manner. Please remember on reading the following five chapters that if what has been written so far at all appeals to you, then the idea of objective morality should also appeal. It is doubtful you will agree with all five of these areas, but this is what morality is all about and where society has gone drastically wrong. There are right answers to be had and it is our responsibility to change our minds and amend our lifestyles accordingly. We ought to be rational, and adjustments to this may very well mean initial struggles to start being rational, rather than stubbornly decrying truth, facts and the relative nature of morality. Just like a good scientist doesn't cast the same theory over and over as correct in spite of evidence, a good person doesn't ignore moral logic in favour of short term, comforting ignorance. Remain critical and rational, but always open minded to new evidence. And as I said before, like we all wish to do, prioritise rational perspective over hard wired intuitions as much as possible. It's moral quandaries in which we see our own comfort challenged in the pursuit of fairness and truth that we can experience a small fraction of what is was like to be Darwin discovering an unpleasant fact about why humans exist, or Galileo realising that he had evidence to contradict a 1000 year old tradition. All be it only a small fraction, some might still say that discovering truth which disagrees with your own conventions is even more difficult than disagreeing with the powers in society. In this sense one can feel alive and liberated in freeing themselves from personal dogma, whilst owing a debt of gratitude to the great minds that allowed for a society where we can practice such freedom of opinion.

Never the less, just as dead pan honesty might be required as to your current beliefs, a healthy dose of scepticism is encouraged. A scientific theory of morality is not about what I decide is right, any more than physics is about what any one physicist discovers. These five chapters which follow are my thoughts as to the current state of things; thoughts that I hope are backed by strong arguments and evidence where required, but that I freely admit I may be wrong about. In essence they mark nothing more than what should be the beginning of study in the new discipline of moral science. Given science's wonderful ability to develop and improve, I am as sure that at least one of my thoughts will be wrong as I am that several of them will prove controversial. But then admitting this is the beauty of science. Let the evidence lead the way.

RATIONALITY

I doubt the first section of practical application will come as any surprise: rationality. Yet this is not something that we, as human beings, have a proud history of accepting. Indeed, rational people are wrongly stereotyped as being cold, calculating machines even though nothing could be further from the truth. Just like selfish acts are rationally thought out, so are kind acts and compassionate acts. Indeed, explicit selfish acts tend to be thought out by those who are misinterpreting rationality; people who only care about themselves, and act with a sentimental view of basic instinct rather than complex rational analysis. Whereas kind and compassionate acts are often the preserve of people who know they have enough security so are willing to impart some of it onto others. Not always, but often enough to allow a generalisation I hope.

A rational, truthful theory of morality involves an acceptance that we ought to be rational. I explained this early on, as it's the crux of theory. We are rational creatures and, as much as we may often find misplaced comfort in ignorance and hearsay, we are doomed/blessed (delete as appropriate) to consider decisions in a rational manner whether we like it or not. Indeed, there has yet to be any believable proof that any human being is, or ever has been, capable of making decisions on a non-rational basis. We sum up decisions in our minds, and act on the basis of our genes and our personalities, which are entirely constitutive of who we are. At no point do we act randomly or make choices we believe are irrational. We may act irrationally in every decision we make, but this doesn't mean the process of deciding how to act was ever random or non-rational in nature. At worst, we can be bad judges of external rationality, but we are never irrationally-able in the sense that I have explained it.

Just as simply as the theory proposes rationality as the meaning in our lives, or more accurately, as the way our lives do function and the way they have to continue to do so whether we like it or not, falling in line with a consistent theory of morality (one which takes a strong, fact based position like other sciences do) involves starting to value rationality as a societal matter as well as one of our natural capabilities. We will never be able to get away from our rational instincts, they underpin everything we do, and ignoring this in society is simply holding back our ability to find truth in traditionally non-scientific areas. Valuing rationality and everything it stands for—namely consistency—helps to foster a society where evidence, improvement, morality and respect are primary and where tradition, superstition, faith and prejudice are held to be merely occurrences which need singling out and discarding when they are found to be opposing reason. Of course there is no reason to value something simply because it is natural for us to do so, but rationality isn't like other natural characteristics: making decisions based on truth and reality across the board is not something to be avoided, so why cage such a natural ability?

Indeed, we can describe emotions which we infer are generally morally significant (like 'kindness', 'compassion', 'evil' and 'selfishness') by reference to rationality. After all, it is a rational process in our mind that determined we should act in this way. Thereby, rather than simply judging an action as 'kind', we can judge how rational it was as a factual matter. This does not mean saying 'Yes it was rational, as he decided to be kind and every decision is the result of a rational process.' but rather 'Was it rational to exhibit kindness in that situation?' If it was in a situation during which one person had easily enough time or resources to exhibit kindness, and the other person was helped in some way by that decision—or indeed society was helped by it, as it fostered more of a respect for the emotion of kindness, which was needed as society was overtly selfish in nature—then it would seem to be rational. Alternatively, if a person starved because of being kind, whilst the recipient had more than enough, and society as a general rule was already being overly 'kind' in nature, then it was not a rational choice to make. This is what we need to be wary of: absurd moral rules which preach irrational ideas. Rationality is not in the business of these sorts of abstract principles.

This individual explanation of circumstance is used to illustrate the point that kindness can be as irrational (and thereby immoral) as selfishness, and that selfishness can be as moral as kindness. The two are rationally formed and are rational responses to different situations. Most probably the reason we deem kindness entirely positively and selfishness entirely negatively is due to religious rules on it, preaching a kind of martyrdom. A rational version of morality doesn't allow the self to be exploited at the expense of others, any more than vice versa. Of course, these examples are only individual cases, and in a society with millions of people, where the inhabitants are not rational machines, it makes no sense to judge it unnecessary to have general moral rules about kindness or selfishness. As discussed at length earlier, we need rules precisely because we are not rational machines. However the explanation is necessary to show that there is no overarching rule whereby kindness is positive and selfishness is negative, instead they both play important roles in rationality and in morality. Neither is the solution, nor is either the problem and hence this theory disagrees with the crux of many moral theories which judge at an aesthetic level that they are. Rationality is the solution.

The reason I make this point is to make one thing clear: rationality is not just important after we attribute moral rules around kindness or respect, it is important in discovering those rules in the first place. It makes no sense to say, like

Pinker does, that reason has extended empathy, which in turn has made society better for everyone (and so assuming we needed empathy first). Rather, what Pinker's important, practical analysis shows is that as we've become more rational, more empathy has been forthcoming as a result of this, and so society has become more civilised. Rationality is the increasing factor that has improved society. The old argument that rational decisions are cold and unforgiving is nonsense and holds no more water than the argument that spiritualists are better people than non spiritualists[63]. We need to ditch these sorts of myths in order to progress into discovering real meaning. Accepting rationality and using reason is how we prove these myths wrong, and it's also how we progress with morality.

ATHEISM

As surely as morality requires rationality in order to be sound, our valuing of rationality can't be done in tandem with a valuation that belief in spite of evidence is acceptable.

Many claim that religious people can make rational decisions in other areas, so attacking 'faith' is flawed. Of course they can, but this misses the point somewhat. We can all think rationally and only rationally in that sense, religion does nothing to change this in any individual. Thus the problem is not necessarily with our rational capabilities being diminished, but more with our rational intentions being reduced.

---

[63] A good few studies, as mentioned earlier, show that spiritualists give more to charity, however this doesn't make them better people. Indeed it is the rational side of them, the side that believes that either they are gaining or will gain something from the giving, that compels them to give to charity a greater amount. The fact rationalists also give money to charity at all would be an argument that they are better people, as they believe no God or cosmic force is benefitting them by doing so. In truth, both are just as decent and as rational morality is taken on board we should see people being more rational and more charitable as a whole (though this doesn't necessarily mean giving money away, so much as making more charitable decisions), all be it more wary of poor charity ideas as also earlier mentioned. A reduction in the number of charities there are would also be a good, and hopefully predictable, sign.

Consider the very worst example of religious dogmatism — extremist terrorism. A man wears a smile, happy in the knowledge that he and his family are going to a fulfilling afterlife, as he is about to fly a plane full of innocent people into a tower also full of innocent people. If one looks at the psychological processes going on inside the man's head, it should become obvious that at no point is he making a decision which he believes to be irrational, or which is indeed formed irrationally. Given what he believes is true, what he is doing makes perfect sense. He believes God sets moral facts, that what he is doing is moral rather than immoral, and that he will be eternally rewarded for it. The problem is not that he reasons in an irrational manner, it's that he believes things with more assumptions than 'we ought to be rational'. His faith-based personal truths are no more than dangerous, taught delusions. There's no valuing of solid evidence there, and either he, or else the culture he lives in, has developed a respect for forming decisions in a dangerously irrational manner simply because they do not ask for evidence.

No one believes religion wholly consists of people willing to go to these extremes. However, it highlights exactly where the problem with religious thinking is. The problem is not that the rational capabilities of human beings in societies that value faith are reduced, it is more that the valuing of what constitutes 'facts' and 'evidence' is astoundingly irrational or non-existent, and that intentions to act and decide rational outcomes are reduced. The rational process is as fine as in any other human being (if slightly underused and under-nurtured), the threat to public security comes with the ideas that valuing faith, and forming beliefs without evidence, are profoundly acceptable ways to think and judge truth. Generally in society we understand that delusions are dangerous, and we should be consistent with this rational understanding no matter how culturally ingrained the delusion.[64] The argu-

---

[64] One will recognise the similarity to Harris' own arguments on this matter from *The End of Faith* and many of his other works. His influence is neither hidden nor accidental, and his work on this subject, along with Dawkins, is truly pioneering.

ments against this criticism, which are now forthcoming from many quarters, are many, but all are lacking:

Not all religious people are terrorists

No, they certainly aren't, no one would claim something so preposterously untrue. As someone who grew up in a small community centred by a beautiful church, I can attest to the fact that people weren't running around violently threatening nonbelievers nor disregarding the rights of others. But what does that prove? It shows that rationality, and its great pull on our minds, is enough to fight much faith-based dogmatism. As society becomes more secular (which itself shows we naturally tend toward rationality *anyway*), nonsensical laws such as blasphemy have been dropped, as people no longer see it as important. Indeed, people rarely now hold witch trials or cat burnings either. Faith is diminishing in value in society, and so is irrationality, wholesale. Many of those people where I grew up might have been believers, but you can bet that when encountering each other on the streets and stopping for a chat, or helping one another out with some task, they were not doing so on pain of punishment from God if they didn't. They were genuine and good people, and they believed in community. Had they been the types that needed the threat of divine punishment, it is difficult to imagine that they would have been quite so nice to one another.

This is an argument for further secularisation, as taking away that valuation of faith-based thinking is necessary in science if we want truth, as it reduces the ability for people to act unscientifically and prove things which aren't true. Similarly, once we view morality as an aspect of rational thinking, we also see a parallel need to reduce valuation of faith-based beliefs. Just as science wouldn't accept arguments attributed to God, society shouldn't accept them either. If morality is to be objective, it also needs to be rational.

Religion isn't irrational

So comes the classic claims of pre-enlightenment society rearing their ugly heads once again: *one cannot prove God doesn't exist, so it is not irrational to believe in him.* If one believes this is a good argument, one can't outwardly value science or rational arguments in the first place. Science never proves things 100% beyond doubt, truth simply doesn't work this way. There is always the possibility that a fact or a belief could be wrong upon discovery of new evidence. This doesn't make believing in things without evidence, or being unsure in spite of no evidence, a valid position. Indeed, making up statements with no evidence (God exists/the Easter bunny exists/gravity is just invisible jelly) does not make them true, or more true than ideas which haven't been said out loud. We must remember that *clarification on what nonsense entails doesn't make it any less nonsense.* And the idea of God is, however you look at it, utter nonsense.

I couldn't scientifically claim gravity was "a theory just as valid as invisible, strong jelly that pulls us to the Earth" because such an idea is hearsay with no evidence to back it up. I also couldn't rationally espouse racism as correct, believing whites to be supremely genetically different to people with other colours of skin. One doesn't have to be unsure about racism any more than one has to be unsure about invisible jelly or God. All are equally baseless in claim and neither could be considered justifiable positions, or indeed sound agnostic middle grounds, as there is definite favour for one side of the argument. Supporting agnosticism in these areas is decidedly irrational and inconsistent if we want to believe facts or truths exist at all.

The esteemed Professor Stephen Hawking explains the argument against religion in a way that sums it up nicely. He argues that *physics leaves no room for God.*[65] If there is no evidence for God, and there is no space for an explanation

---

[65] The Grand Design: New Answers to the Ultimate Questions of Life. *Stephen Hawking and Leonard Mlodinow.*

such as God in our understanding of the universe, then God is nothing more than a failed hypothesis. The inventor of the phrase 'New Atheism', Victor J. Stenger, has written extensively on this topic, and indeed he argues that given the religious hypothesis about God, we should have expected to see a variety of evidence for his existence, when in actual fact there is none. The book he wrote is called, unflinchingly and unsurprisingly, *God: The Failed Hypothesis*. Arguments in favour of God dwell on the single idea that the burden of proof is on atheists, and yet they fail to note many other aspects of truth finding as Stenger has, or as I have briefly explained here.

Science can tell us how but not why, so religion/spirituality is fact finding of a different kind

Many people in modern society take this stance and admit facts of science as readily as they admit that religious/spiritual reasoning is needed to give us meaning, or explain why we are here. But how is this any different to the previous claim that religion isn't irrational?

Consider that I make up a new religion tomorrow as an experiment. I have no truth or experiences to base it on, I simply start an on-line campaign to show that the meaning of our lives is to touch-type as fast as possible. There is a typing angel who watches over us, I claim, who created us all out of Times New Roman and destined us to make keyboards in order to reach our hidden potential. Perhaps we could even find our 'inner letter' by doing this. Despite the fact I had no evidence and no experiential truth, would this be a relevant form of investigation into why we are here? Similarly, would our 'inner letter' be a sensible concept just because I had uttered the proposition regarding it? I will repeat my simple sentiments from earlier in response: *clarification on what nonsense entails doesn't make it any less nonsense.* There is an unlimited amount of nonsense you could cobble together, and uttering one piece of it out loud doesn't suddenly make it truer than the infinite amount of nonsense that no one has ever uttered. When nonsense becomes culturally ingrained, it doesn't seem as silly as analogies like 'typing angels', but if you look at the logic there is no difference in evidence.

Science in fact has a perfectly good explanation of why we are here: we evolved. There was probably no creator at all and we just happened into existence after millions of years of evolution, and years before that of universal development which itself sparks from stellar events of what we believe was a phenomena called the 'big bang'. An event in which space and time was created. Can we know how something can pop into existence from nothing? Not at the moment, as far as I can see, and physicists are beginning to argue that this is down to our misapprehending how time works (as time itself seems to have been invented when the big bang occurred, so there was nothing before; thus they argue that the question doesn't make sense). However unintuitive we find these arguments in physics, this doesn't mean that if I make up ideas, or take on board ideas from cultural definitions of God figures or 'experience', then it is likely to help in answering these questions. Once again: *clarifying what nonsense entails doesn't make it any less nonsense.*

In fact, that latter nonsensical supposition (that 'experience' has a truth value of its own) is perhaps the most intuitive pull that this entire pro-religion argument has: the idea that science can measure and find truths in certain areas, but that to find truth on a meaningful level we need to look 'within ourselves' and find 'experiential truths' that science isn't capable of finding. Yet we have evolved from other primates (we still are primates, in fact), and at different points in history our ancestors have been in biological vehicles of various proportions going right back to single celled organisms in primordial broth. Does it make sense to say that the meaning of an amoeba is for it to look inside of itself and find the 'why am I here?' Does it make sense that rats are missing out because they can only think from their own instincts, and can't decide not to eat today because they are contemplating how to find real meaning in their lives? Put next to the understanding of a scientific theory like evolution, 'why questions' like the above seem to miss the point of what rationality is. All sentient individuals have some sort of rational mental mechanism helping them in their attempts to survive (not on the level of being able to create civilised science, or organised societies like we can, although species like ants appear to come closest), yet none appear to have the ability to 'find truth from looking within'. Indeed, as an evolutionary matter, it makes sense to say that spiritual questions like this are misplaced rationality from a species who has grown so rationally capable, into such efficient, effective societies that it is has time to ask needless questions or create ways of trying to outwit its own rationality. Further irony, perhaps? We can find meaning in an infinite number of ways that do not involve making spiritual and faith based ideas up, one wonders why it is that we are so desperate to escape the wonder of reality.

SPIRITUALITY CAN BE EXPLAINED

To finish off this section, which has argued throughout that rationality and atheism are necessary, morally important concepts, one has to take on board this final point which has just been alluded to: spirituality, far from being a good method of finding meaning, is rationally explainable as a flawed hypothesis.

This is important, as no matter how many arguments are made against spirituality as a rational matter, there are still human beings who want to find meaning in it. They want to believe in the magical, or mythical, and a society which values faith (which our current society does) is one that gives people justification for continuing to listen to spiritual ideas in an act of unnecessary hope. Explaining spirituality for what it is may be the key in unlocking the rational ability of our society to discard faith and all the danger it entails.

So, consider the points I have made throughout this book so far. Human beings are unique in their rational capabilities. We can rationally attain our needs, we have evolved better and better able to do this, and are at the stage where we can consciously evolve our society in an instant (or at least in a few months or years) rather than having to wait many generations like in most examples of evolutionary biology in other species. We have thus attained a desire to search, continuously and entirely naturally, for ways of finding more truths; ways of seeking more and faster advancement.

Institutional science is an especially important and effective way of doing this, valuing, as it does, evidence, checks, the ability to repeat results and the humility to admit it is wrong on facts where evidence becomes available that said facts were incorrect. I have argued that spirituality is the enemy of this, as it seeks to have us accept truths without evidence, and as Dawkins argues, to "be satisfied with not understanding the world"[66] However, I have also argued that we each, however much we try to avoid it, have an innate way of thinking which is based on rational decision making. As such, spirituality can be defined as the erroneous, misplaced desire to be rational without a full understanding of what science and rationality involves.

And this is by no means a slight on religious or spiritual people, who I fully admit are striving for answers in ways they perceive to be rational. Some are also extremely capable in certain areas of science. Many scientists are often keen to note that they can't answer the "big questions" and so take faith erroneously in ideas which are neither supported by evidence nor backed up in the way which a rational outlook would require. This shows us that many scientists *themselves* are often unfortunate products of a society in which faith is entirely misunderstood to be a valid way of finding rational answers. This further tells us that many scientists don't understand the great importance of their roles, viewing them simply in immediately functional terms. This is no great shock. Wanting to answer a 'why are we here?' type question is incredibly compelling, and difficult to see as the

---

[66] Quoted from the documentary entitled 'Enemies of Reason' originally aired on UK based Channel 4.

nonsensical question it is for most people, who do not realise that the very question assumes the meaning that it is meant to be asking about, and thus is nothing more than illogical hyperbole. This brings us to the final point in this chapter.

Faith is the problem

The problem is not people comforting themselves near death with a belief in an afterlife, or people looking to the teachings of Jesus for moral guidance (though this latter point may be mistaken, as the Christian author CS Lewis noted, "You can shut him up for a fool, you can spit at him and kill him as a demon, or you can fall at his feet and call him Lord and God. But let us not come with any patronizing nonsense about his being a great moral teacher. He has not left that open to us."[67]). Neither is the problem scientists not knowing the answers to what we think are the "big questions", which might simply be the questions of a species who don't understand the nature of what answers are meant to be, or how to tell an important question from one which assumes a concept which can't possibly exist. The moral problem is that we aren't educated to value rationality.

The fact we see answers based around nothing but a 'faith', or even that we see the attitude of having 'faith' as a positive, moral way of reasoning, shows we haven't understood what faith is. We are human beings; individuals evolved from a variety of other organisms, but still just organisms. No doubt consciousness causes us problems in science, as it asks diffi-cult questions akin to the other great scientific investigations in history (many of which we have now solved, by the way: most of our previous "evidence" for God and the spiritual is now explained; from solar and lunar eclipses, to weather systems and the inner workings of the human body). But the fact we can rationalise things in a way that's unique in the animal kingdom does not make us special, and the fact that we are so efficient that we have time on our hands does not

---

[67] Mere Christianity. *C.S. Lewis.*

mean that questions we posit demand answers that science and rationality cannot provide. Perhaps, as I've shown, the questions themselves only make sense as a grammatical matter. We invented grammatical rules, and they work well most of the time, but they do not necessarily guarantee that a question makes sense as a logical matter.

Faith asks people not only to be satisfied with not understanding (thus asking them to throw their support behind fairy tales), but it also asks people to forgo decisions that are made with evidence and reason in relation to reality, for those that are made through the same rational mental processes but with no such evidence or reasoning. What's worse is that we don't just use faith to answer personal questions that reason cannot yet answer, or to answer questions that themselves don't make sense, we also employ faith in politics, sometimes in science, and most problematically in judging whether acts are moral or immoral. Faith is simply not to be taken seriously in areas where objective facts are important. And furthermore it is credible to note that a society that stands for faith at all, valuing as it does the ideas which oppose rationality, will cultivate the same society that feels no need for rational consistency. This doesn't just mean we see blunted science, with many not interested in answers, but we also see a society with a stagnating moral compass in which faith and reason are equal, and thus where morality is a subject of personal tastes rather than objective moral consequences.

What this does *not* mean, as a practical matter, is that we should discriminate against those with religious views or incite violence. Being rational is about being fair to people, and this includes those who do not value what is right. However, we need to begin challenging the value of 'faith' wherever it occurs: in people, in institutions and in society as a whole. It's no longer something we can ignore, and with the threat of biological and nuclear weapons of mass destruction, along with an animal population of trillions being decimated each year, faith needs to be cast away from serious discussion for the same reason prejudice is currently being erased. What we need more than anything is people looking to evidence and science for answers, rather than pitting their gods or imaginary 'facts' against one another. The latter could destroy the world, as it isn't open to rational, sensible, evidence based discussion like science is; proponents cannot be proved wrong and so can take things on to an extreme, fatal level. We can no longer pretend faith is the preserve of gentle people when we live in a society where religious terrorism has killed thousands in the last few years alone, and where religion is fighting back for its place in government across the world. The stand needs to be of rationality against *all* faith.

6. *Animal Ethics*

SENTIENCE

Almost all societies have come a long way from the influential Cartesian, flawed understanding of animals as unfeeling machines[68]. Such is further recognition of the useful role science plays that far from viewing animals as machines, or as soulless individuals to be looked down upon, most of us now view animals for what they are: sentient individuals at various places in an evolutionary tree.

Just as humans evolved from singular celled organisms, every animal alive today is also the product of millions of years of rich evolutionary history; history which has created such an array of sentient individuals, that it would take more than anyone's lifetime to understand the complexities of each different species.

As far as morality is concerned though, we need not be directly concerned with single celled organisms, or trees, or plants. We need only concern ourselves with sentient individuals. Throughout I make reference to this, and here seems as good a reason as any to explain it (not that it should require much explaining). To be a subject of moral respect,

---

[68] Discourse on the Method. Descartes, R. 1637.
It has been bought to my attention that the Philosopher John Cottingham has criticised and argued against this widely regarded view that Descartes held animals as nothing more than unfeeling machines. Cottingham has written a paper entitled *'A Brute to the Brutes?': Descartes' Treatment of Animals* in which he examines Descartes writings on this matter, and argues that although he did believe them to be machines, he may well have regarded them as being sentient to some degree. A high amount of scepticism exists within this piece, and it is unlikely to ever be backed up hard evidence either way. For the purposes of my using Descartes' widely attributed view, it matters little whether Descartes actually believed it or not; the view itself was influential and descriptive of an 'unfeeling' toward animals which describes more accurately the historical context of the human view of other animals as opposed to the more sympathetic view we hold today. We can happily call this 'unfeeling' perspective a Cartesian influenced view, either way, as it was influenced and widely attributed to Descartes.

one has to be able to experience one's life. To our best scientific understanding, trees indeed are 'unfeeling machines' by virtue of being organisms that act on non-conscious process, grow and naturally respond to stimuli in all manner of ways. Like rocks, they have no nervous system; nothing central that is conscious and experiences what is happening to them or around them.

We can draw the morally important distinction between conscious and unconscious through science and rationality. We know (as far as we can know) that we are conscious. We can feel pain, we can experience contentment to some degree and we are subjects of our own lives, as the American philosopher Tom Regan might put it[69]. We know that this isn't because we are organic and grow or respond to stimuli (like any organism can), but rather because of our central nervous system which evolves *after* the ability to respond to stimuli. Nerves transmit stimuli which cause pain; a brain experiences the pain and takes the pain on board to tell the nerve to stop experiencing that pain, and thus the process of this emotion acts as a negative feeling to the person experiencing it. In being subjects of lives, rather than organic machines, we experience this as conscious individuals. There is something to experience the reaction (me), rather than just the action happening by itself. That's a basic scientific description of sentience at work. To be sceptical of sentience itself seems more paranoid than sceptical, and indeed we see further evidence and agreement about sentience as a scientific matter every year.[70] This is the norm within the scientific community and within western society.

Upon the scientific realisation that experiencing life is not related to organisms so much as to consciousness (of which concepts like a central nervous system are a marker for: as they transmit messages for a central brain to create a

---

[69] Regan, 1983.
[70] http://fcmconference.org/ This, the Francis Crick Memorial Conference 2012, was the latest development in non-human consciousness, in which a declaration was signed by scientists as renowned as Stephen Hawking in order to fully attest to the idea that non-human consciousness exists.

'sensing' of it), our understanding of evolution comes in handy. We know we evolved from other primate species, so when we look at primates and see a similar biological make up in many ways, it makes sense to start connecting the dots and noting that other individuals that are not human are probably sentient. Indeed it is to advance a 'faith-based' position to state that consciousness appears only once a species has evolved into the human species. The biological similarities and existence of a nervous system in so many other individuals would make such a claim invalid. Simple observation of the facts makes it untenable, and as Voltaire put it many years ago, "People must have renounced, it seems to me, all natural intelligence to dare to advance that animals are but animated machines... It would be very strange that they should express so well what they could not feel."[71] The recognition that animals appear to experience emotions, coupled with our best scientific knowledge of how sentience is marked in our own species, makes it a steadfast fact that at least some animals are sentient. As well as humans and other primates, the group of sentient animals must also include animals with similar biological consistency and physical traits such as cows, pigs, dogs, geese, chickens, birds, many fish, giraffes...the list is almost endless, and we can't know for sure where it stops (for instance some classifications of animals, like sponges, actually appear to be non-sentient; perhaps we also shouldn't rule the idea out that some non-animal organisms can be sentient?)

However we can be fairly sure that most, if not all, animals we generally use in industry and affect in society are sentient. Moreover, it doesn't hurt to be careful. Just as we wouldn't remove lifesaving medication in any normal situation where we weren't sure a human was still a subject of life, or whether he or she had died and so was no longer sentient, we also shouldn't allow ourselves to exploit an

---

[71] Traité sur la Tolérance

individual of another species when we genuinely aren't sure of their sentience.[72] Logical extensions of any rational version of morality would stretch to non-human animals.

We can be rationally assured that many animals are therefore sentient, but why is sentience of moral importance? Why rationally discard those organisms, or physical objects that aren't sentient? Why not extend morality to everything? Well, morality is about wellbeing. Just as the umbrella of health makes no sense when applied to rocks or kettles or flag poles, morality doesn't either. We can show morality to be intensely rational and extending morality to be a consistent move, but we can't show rational reason for extending it to non-sentient organisms or objects as there is no subject of a life in them with which to experience any change in moral treatment. Nothing at all; (as explained earlier) these organisms consist only of movements, with nothing conscious to experience those actions. Morality relates only to 'sensing' organisms, or sentient organisms, for the same reason that biology relates to organic organisms, or geology relates to physical facts and forces.

This entire idea, that non-human animals can be subjects deserving of ethical consideration, should affect us a great deal. As I earlier noted, we can be fairly sure that most of the animals we use in human industry are sentient, amounting to tens of billions of land animals every year and potentially over a trillion aquatic creatures.[73]

---

[72] Of course such a principle, in human or nonhuman relations, could be sacrificed if it were the case that one's life was threatened. For instance, in the event of a plane crash on a remote island it wouldn't necessarily be irrational to kill and eat a rabbit for continued survival if it were all the nourishment that was available, just as it wouldn't be irrational to eat a fellow passenger if he was all that was available.

[73] The Food and Agriculture Organization of the United Nations is the generally used source for statistics on land animals (noting 56 billion land animals per year in 2003), whilst the figures on sea animals is much more difficult to gauge as catches in the oceans are often measured in tons rather than numbers of individual animals. The only known source I could find was as follows (estimating the number of fish as in the region of 1-2 trillion):

http://www.fishcount.org.uk/published/standard/fishcountfullrptSR.pdf)

WELFARISM

It felt odd writing that last chapter, as one wonders if it was really needed. We live in a society where even TV chefs and exploitative tabloid newspapers champion the causes of different non-human animals, so why would I think the reader needed to be encouraged to see that animals are sentient, like us? Consider it more of a self-indulging history lesson to back my ideas rather than something to enlighten you, the reader.

The TV chefs and tabloid media are remarkably good markers of how society feels: transmitting, as they do, the 'safe' norms and values of society so as they don't disintegrate their popularity by alienating their audience. Society, almost as a whole, views animals as individuals with interests. As such it shocks us all to see chickens crammed ten to a tiny cage, or dogs abused by immature or violent owners. Our championing and support of causes related to opposing these sorts of actions speak well of our relinquishing the chains of religious dogmatism that would beg us to believe animals have no interests because God gave them no soul.

However this 'welfarism' from which these campaigns spring (that aim to improve our treatment of animals) is currently counter-productive at best and absolutely irrational at worst. In Chapter 4 I discussed the issue briefly, and the work of Professor Francione who has shown the flaw in its legal process. Welfarism does little for animals but make their exploitation more efficient. As a philosophical matter, welfarism appears to improve little for animals both due to Francione's economic argument that such costs for significant improvement couldn't be taken on board in welfarist campaigns, and because the reasoning behind supposed improvements assumes animals have human feelings that their situation could be 'better or worse'. Welfarism is both economically and psychologically irrational.

Indeed, I characterised Pinker's own analysis of welfarism's great improvements for animals as incorrect because although we are arguably progressing in levels of civility and peace thanks to reason, violence isn't decreasing as we are finding ways to alleviate our consciences with more violence than ever before in the direction of non-human individuals. This is extremely important. Rational morality acknowledges that as we become more rational, society will morally improve. Indeed, Pinker in a roundabout way agrees, stating as he has that 'there has never been a better time to be a potential victim'[74]. However animal use is one of the ways in which we trick ourselves into seeing rational improvement, when in fact we are actually just making irrational claims. Not least because we don't like the idea of challenging ourselves to change anything significant about our lifestyles. This 'speciesism' is so ingrained in our society that even Pinker's analysis in Better Angels of our Nature, which in my mind is one of the greatest academic achievements of the 21st century so far, fails to spot its effect in blunting the good intentions of welfarism.

ANTI-SPECIESISM HAS TO BE THE MORAL BASELINE

When writing the introduction to the 'practical ethics' section of this book, I would be lying if I didn't see the unflinching reason that asks us to start becoming anti-speciesists as the reason why people might immediately start 'philosophising' reasons out of agreeing with me. Rationalists, like everyone else, are desperate not to have to look inward on any subject, and whilst I imagine stating atheism as a moral imperative will still raise a few eyebrows, it is the claim of anti-speciesim which I suspect will bring out the faith-based fear in otherwise rational people. Yet anti-speciesim makes perfect sense: we are not talking about creating a society that see's humans and animals as equally able, it is an entirely different 'ism' in this sense. We simply need to inject rationality to any situations where we indulge prejudice based on species. Anti-speciesim arguably only requires ethical veganism on a personal level, which is the practice of eliminating animal products (as far as is possible) from one's diet and lifestyle.

[74] Taken from his Ted talk, http://www.youtube.com/watch?v=ramBFRt1Uzk. This idea is also alluded to in Pinker, 2011.

No cuddling cows, no joining PETA and no giving dogs a right to vote. And certainly no throwing red paint over people. Just *rational veganism*; which I am well aware might be two words that have never deserved to be read in tandem before. But why do I think we need to go this far, rather than settle with a better form of welfarism?

Welfarism is a hit or miss system of trying to look out for animal interests. Before we even get to the mammoth practical problems with trying to garner rights for individuals who are legally and socially seen as property (as explained in chapter 4), there is one basic irrational flaw in welfarism: the assumption that animals are our products to be used in the first place. We certainly could back animal use on the same grounds that we can back our belief in God. Perhaps even more so, because we eat animals in our meals every day, we wear them on our bodies, we even rub them into our skin. Animal use is perhaps more imbedded into our being than religion is, and as such, the mountain path away from animal use is intertwined with the one of fighting faith. It takes an honest person to point out that animal use is entirely tradition-based and not at all rational, and that eliminating animal use from our lives is not just rationally preferable, it is the very baseline of rational morality given the potential billions of otherwise victims. I stated rational morality wasn't a game of numbers in terms of formulae and equations, but when we are justifying the deaths of trillions of animals every year based purely on our will to continue our traditions and habits, the numbers speak for themselves.

It takes a special kind of monstrous irrationality to oppose the point I am making here. As rationalists it is easy to ignore such a point on the grounds that vegans are traditionally spiritually inclined, tie-dye and sandal wearers, with a penchant for peace signs instead of progress. However those of us who have cast out ideas about God, and created entire movements opposing theism and encouraging skepticism about the paranormal, are better placed than most to see through the social stigma. We are also more rationally able to see the problems with the industry approved system of welfarism.

I don't need to explain the hideous uses of animals we indulge ourselves in yearly, and neither will I go into them. You can find the horrific pictures and videos of all types of animal use in various places, so I've no need to waste your time here. If one wants to make claims that the supposedly humane use of cows, pigs, chickens, fish, etc., anywhere on Earth justifies our choosing meat, dairy, eggs or leather, for example (many other types of animal use exist), rather than something non-animal-based when shopping, then let's not delude ourselves. No one reading this is naïve enough to think this is a sound argument, or one which their 'neutral rationality' is pointing to; we use animals primarily out of taste, and it is very difficult to rationally justify any kind of death or suffering (however humane in comparison to even worse killing or suffering) by holding our tastes on a pedestal. Rather, our use of animals is entirely needless. There's little if anything we need to use them for, and as decent, rational people it's time we really started to think decently and rationally. There is probably no God, and there's definitely no reason we can't walk past the butcher's section in the supermarket. If the effort of a little thought and care by the consumer is not morally outweighed by the immense suffering and eventual early deaths of billions of entirely sentient individuals every year then we simply are not looking at the evidence in the right way. There is no moral fact as solid as this one, as far as I can see. Welfarism, in all its current forms, has failed and could never balance the equation between taste and death. It may well be time to create a movement for *rational anti-speciesism* or *rational veganism*.

DELETING THE 'MORAL CONTRACT' THESIS

There's one very intuitive criticism of stating anti-speciesim as a moral baseline. I have stated throughout that morality is rational as it serves us well. We ought to be rational, as being rational not only means we get truth rather than personal opinion (as irrationality 'fudges' results), but as a practical matter it naturally asks us to go and create a better world for everyone by virtue of not allowing for risks that you might be one of the victims of a world where victims are common place: reducing the number of victims reduces the risk of you being one. Rational morality includes altruism that thus happens to be self-serving as well as entirely rational and scientific. This is, I believe, one of the great practical strengths of the theory.

This undoubtedly brings up an important issue. Animals are not party to respecting this morality and cannot intellectually follow moral laws, so why should they be included at all? There appears to be no benefit to us. This criticism is intuitive because it views morality as that selfish, rational tool; perhaps one that I have exploited by stating the practical benefits of my theory. However, as I've explained, the pragmatics are not the primary thing. Once we accept morality as a rational discipline, like we accept physics as a rational discipline for understanding and improving our world, then it becomes a case of making it rational. We don't 'fudge' the results in physics and plump for answers simply because they serve us well[75], so why would we fudge the results in morality just because it serves us better? That's not morality, that's just exercising selfish will.

Moral science, once accepted as a discipline of rationality like the others (physics, maths, biology, etc), which is the only way we can usefully accept it, becomes constitutive of the same rules. If one area is useful for advancing our world then it becomes a case of rationality. The same goes for them all equally, else we are doing precisely what the moral relativist

---

[75] Of course, one might argue we do fudge results in physics to some degree, by only exploring those fields which are useful to us to explore. My point with the analogy, though, is that we don't just change the figures; indeed we couldn't else we would shoot ourselves in the foot as our theories wouldn't work. Physics by definition cannot generally fudge results. However if there were examples where physicists could just make up ideas, it would certainly be looked down upon. Indeed those who try to fudge quantum mechanics results by twisting them to seemingly prove spiritual positions could be said to be fudging results. Such 'woo' is looked down upon by physicists and seen to be devaluing the subject, rather than being given any sort of truth value.

does in judging morality to be subjective and useful only as a pragmatic matter individually, or what the spiritualist does in judging truths where there is no evidence. It may be true that morality evolved as a sort of moral contract, but that doesn't mean we must persist with it as such, for the same reason that if physics developed as a way of worshipping and under-standing God's creation, it doesn't have to continue as such.

However, there is still a practical relevance; one that has been with us for many years and that is on my side. Kant explained the necessity to be 'kind' to animals in purely anthropocentric terms, he didn't believe animals themselves had interests, as he didn't view them as rational[76]. He believed that we should be kind to animals as it fosters respect to each other as humans. Indeed, some modern day studies back this up and show that violent criminals often have a history of abusing animals[77]. As the psychologist Bradley Millar is credited for saying, "Teaching a child not to step on a caterpillar is as valuable to the child as it is to the caterpillar."[78] In essence, what is being referred to is the idea that animals are sentient individuals: they can be caused pain, and they can even show it in remarkably understandable ways to us humans. Teaching people to ignore this expression of pain and to see it as a necessary part of their own life is an astoundingly easy way to make people numb to the moral pull which sentience naturally has on us. It assists people in ignoring it in humans and in ignoring our rational ability to perceive it. This doesn't seem too far off as an idea, and as much as we need more evidence to put this point into practice, it must still give hope that even the most selfish among us will respect the ideal of anti-speciesism as well as the more scientific or rational among us.

Society currently tries to evade this potential problem by hiding away slaughterhouses and employing lower class

---

[76] *The Metaphysics of Morals*, Immanuel Kant, 1797.

[77] https://www.ncjrs.gov/pdffiles1/ojjdp/188677.pdf

[78] This is another credit, but unsure of the source validity. In any case, it once again is the proposition I want to allude to rather than using the source as proof, so I don't hesitate in using it.

individuals to be the ones causing the suffering on our behalf. We even hide the realities of farming from our children with the same ferocity that we hide violent movies, or the details of immoral murders. But are we really hidden from it, and can we ever be? It seems to me that we naturally want to 'know' where our food comes from and it also seems illiberal for governments to try to hide this for 'our own good', as well as being an instance of irrationally fudging results. Furthermore, it seems to breed faith-based irrational thinking to try to teach children that they must respect other people by virtue of their sentience and ability to experience life, but that they can ignore sentient subjects of a life in other biological categories: this is arbitrary rule setting of the type which we abhor when done in science, or in other areas of life.

The practical aspects of animal use, however briefly considered, may be significant. We seem to naturally react to the sentience of others (we evolved as social creatures, so it would be strange that we wouldn't), and teaching people that it isn't sentience but rather the category of 'being human' that should be respected, appears to be missing something rather important.[79] But in any case, we have to remember that science isn't about practicalities; they are nice to have, but the goal is consistent truth finding.

---

[79] It is not just society that preaches that human beings are the markers of respect, even the human rights campaign group Amnesty International for many years hosted the slogan 'Protect the Human'. For a long time I've seen problems with this slogan, judging as it does that same 'independent moral fact' theory that humans 'just are' what is important to look after. I have never been comfortable with rules without understanding or evidence, and my experiences of amnesty volunteers who could not grasp why I am vegan, or the reasons for 'sentience' rather than 'human' being the marker of moral interests, were probably perhaps the earliest catalysts for the theory of rational morality. It is fitting they should be alluded to at some point, and fitting also that it be mentioned they do an awful lot of good work for human beings; work which I mostly do not oppose, of course.

REMOVING PREJUDICE

Racism, sexism, homophobia...there are many forms of prejudice still strong in the world. Speciesism is one of a different type, but is prejudice in kind all the same. Just as it's irrational to discriminate arbitrarily based on race or sex, it is irrational to discriminate arbitrarily based on species. Just as we don't want to teach our kids to think in terms of justifying irrational prejudice, we adults shouldn't think in those terms either. Progression involves rooting out these kinds of opinions.

Speciesism looks a lot different to known, accepted prejudices because it involves nonhumans. Normal claims of prejudice are often invoked upon the violation of human rights, like to not be given the vote, or to be denied freedom to travel to certain areas. We've no need to put animals into this kind of legal framework. We need just give them one right, as Francione suggests, the right not to be used as property. By doing this we avoid the difficult if not impossible talk about 'manslaughter' of insects when we go running on grassy fields, and we also avoid odd ideas like having to make other animals 'people' in the same way humans are seen (useful if not only because it would be very difficult to discourage the apathy of dogs in general electoral votes). A right not to be used as property is simply a common sense, rational attribution that a sentient individual is not a piece of property and thus has interests. Thereby we shouldn't be attributing ownership over them in the first place. This means nothing more than leaving them alone most of the time. We can't pretend we know what they want, or even how they feel in any profound manner, but we can know that they experience suffering and would be better off without it. Allowing them a right not to be used as property is a simple legal safeguard against the use of animals in industry, or in any behaviour which would attempt to use them as a target of human exploitation. This is simple, rational anti-speciesism at work. As a personal matter it involves the recognition of the importance of being a dietary (at least) vegan, and the abstention from consuming animal products oneself. Perhaps also the adopting of the victims of our current pet or farming systems. In many years (undoubtedly not in our lifetimes), one would like to see the legal part of the theory become relevant also.

MOUNTAINEERING THE ACADEMIC ALPS

Advocating anything involving veganism in the current academic climate might seem analogous to advocating evolution in the time of Darwin. And yet, the basis is there for all to see. Dawkins speaks of the irrational nature of speciesism way back in the 70's in *The Selfish Gene*, and Harris' pioneering ideas in *The Moral Landscape* note that it is the wellbeing of *sentient individuals* and not just humans that matter. The most rational conclusion is to discard this irrational idea that animals are naturally our property in the first place.

Nevertheless, one feels compelled to lay myths out on the table here and now to stop them where they start. The following are all irrational ways to palm off the moral obligation that veganism involves. A good deal of well natured skepticism is required.

Veganism is not healthy, natural or convenient

There exist millions of vegans in the world, and indeed many cultures throughout history have forgone meat regularly, whilst a reliance on eggs and dairy is about as unnatural as any food stuff one could think of; factory processed foods certainly look a lot better when you consider the factories for eggs and milk are the innards of farmyard animals. The Western world's influence is the factor which has recently pushed countries like India and China in particular away from largely vegan based-diets[80]. Vegan diets (though not known as 'vegan' in any area until the 1950s when Donald Watson coined the term) have probably always existed somewhere, and they have been able

---

[80] Resisting the Globalization of Speciesism: Vegan Abolitionism as a Site for Consumer-Based Social Change. Wrenn, C. L. 2011.

to as there exists no nutrient that one can only gain from animal products. It is a distinct bias from our own cultures that allows us to see the vast importance of foods like green vegetables, without also seeing that foods like meat and dairy do not contain anything particularly unique or special. And indeed, it is a profound (and in some sense understandable, up to now) ignorance that stops us from obtaining the evidence that unveils the truth.

Calcium exists in much higher proportions from sources like green vegetables, or even soya beans than it does in dairy. 'Protein-deficiency' is something one could only realistically suffer from whilst starving to death (one could eat only potatoes and not be deficient in protein). Iron, Omega 3 and Iodine can all be catered for in abundance (despite advertisements and schemes run from animal industry stating the opposite). The mysterious vitamin B12 (of which theories suggest we either evolved a need for by gaining its advantages via eating unwashed plant foods or the liver of some animals) can be created in reliable sources in labs and fortified into almost anything we eat. Whilst vitamin D, a nutrient that most of us don't get enough of in any diet (including in vegan diets), is easily catered for vegans and non-vegans alike via vegan supplements, instead of the non-vegan supplements that most people in countries like the UK (with its limited months of quality sunlight) should be taking.

Indeed, one wonders whether the claim of veganism being unhealthy is really believed at all. More importantly, people tend to believe that veganism is either unnatural or inconvenient — two claims holding slightly more believability. Yet, unnatural? As a claim from a species that has flown to the moon, created towering buildings in super cities and managed to both trawl the depths of the deepest seas and fly to the highest points in the atmosphere, one wonders whether we really should judge the usefulness of an action by its relation to being natural. While on the other hand, everything we can do is natural as we are animals, and some things which are entirely natural in others species (like infanticide and the killing of sexual partners) or were common in early versions our own species (like rape or genocide) are not judged moral by their value of being natural. Nature does not judge morality well and can only ever be ambiguous in moral claims. Hence we often value 'being natural' well below the value of 'being immoral', so such an argument should have little say on the subject of veganism.

Inconvenience, then? One can't argue with that for solid reasoning, veganism is certainly more inconvenient at current than non-veganism. And yet one could say the same thing about many social injustices in the past. It was once much easier to partake in all kinds of things than to oppose them (the oppression of women in Europe throughout history and the fascism of Nazi Germany in the 1930's to name but two). And yet many did oppose them, and we like to think we still would. Furthermore, choosing to ignore buying products that have been made via chaining animals up or killing them is hardly going to require the same bravery as opposing a Nazi state or a patriarchal Tudor monarch (either of which could easily result in your murder). A bit of perspective wouldn't go amiss. If moral progress didn't involve changing lifestyles or opinions of some degree, then it wouldn't be moral progress in the first place. For most of us, we are talking about buying something different in a shop, or cooking something different in our homes. As moral choices go, this is as easy as they come.

It seems accurate to label our inability to see veganism as relatively easy, to itself be a product of extremely irrational thinking. It's inconvenient, occasionally, to choose to be vegan only because more people haven't done it. Whether we like it or not we live in a capitalist society, where supply changes (based on the demand) in an effort to make as much money as possible. If people demanded vegan products and refused to buy animal products, supply would change rapidly (we already see most major brands supplying vegan products simply because they are normally made without animal products). And moreover, being vegan is not particularly hard. Picking up vegetables, beans or vegan alternatives ('meats' made from plant sources rather than animal flesh) in a supermarket, instead of picking up eggs or meat, is hardly going to put a strain on one's life. Our initial thought (that veganism is just something we cannot even consider) is a product of the faith-based ideals that work so well at keeping society from advancing. In the same way that faith stops people appreciating truth and the way the world works, it stops people from seeing that same thirst for truth in moral terms, and instead encourages irrational prejudice like speciesism as something they 'need' to do. In this faith-based system, current 'tastes' become an insurmountable opinion one can't change.

FLEXITARIANISM: THE UTILITARIAN POSITION STRIKES AGAIN

As if welfarism wasn't bad enough, flexitarianism also refers to the kinds of positions taken by the likes of the philosopher Peter Singer when referring to animal use. A flexitarian doesn't see veganism as the ideal, but rather as one of many ways to reduce animal suffering. As such veganism may be discarded in a pragmatic manner like when at a restaurant and served cheese accidentally, or for the pleasure of purposefully eating steak occasionally. It may make much more sense for someone like Singer to just eat the cheese or steak, contributing to a greater overall happiness at the dinner table, so as to make veganism seem more pleasant or likeable.

Again, we see the fallacy of shallow pragmatism here. Positions like Singer's do not seem to understand social movements in the slightest. This won't just make the 'vegan' in question seem pleasant and easy, it will also make them seem inconsistent[81], and will make veganism seem like an

---

[81] All-or-Nothing Games in the Civil Rights Movement. Social Science Information 30: 677-697. Chong, D. 1991. Chong shows that collective "goods" can be destroyed by a single compromise, which is very similar to the situation with veganism. Whilst Chong is focusing on protesting events in the civil rights movement, it is easy to draw similarities to the vegan education cause, where 'defectors' like Singer can cause huge problems for many important aspects of vegan education.

unimportant decision to be waded in and out of as one wishes and finds easy to do; pushing those same norms about morality being personal and taste-based which we have identified is the problem, not the solution. One should never compare immoral events, for fear of offense, however would an easy going anti-rapist be bettered served occasionally indulging in rape in order to seem more accessible? We already have an idea that flexitarianism doesn't work in moral theory before we even start speaking about animals.

Furthermore, social movements work like snowballs. The movement against animal use can only do the same: people will reject animals use, or accept it. Positions like flexitarianism ('veganism occasionally'), or even like welfarism itself ('animal use is okay'), take the focus away from what is right (anti-speciesism) and make it look instead like there are several right answers. Each 'right answer' equally valid as a personal choice, and thus the perceived easiest ones will flourish, and the perceived hardest ones will be left to stagnate. Similarly, if these are all right answers, why can't most people reason that their own answer of 'do nothing, but act concerned in social situations' as equally right? Society already changed their opinions from 'animals have no sentience' to 'animals deserve some interests', and yet we appear to exploit more animals now than ever before. Even with a growing world population, the figure is still significant enough that this is still a definite sign of evidence against ideas like flexitarianism.

Veganism is the rational choice with regards to animal ethics, and yet it will always look harder than 'veganism when I feel like it' or 'non-veganism but occasionally buy animal products with a nicer looking label' or more appropriately 'do nothing, but feign concern'. The movement against animal use can only progress like any other social movement in history, picking up speed as it gathers momentum by getting more people on side. And yet, what the likes of Singer's positions do is to take support away from the growing snowball, providing justification for not joining the movement at all. Flexitarianism and welfarism provide the same effect to anti-speciesism that spirituality and agnosticism do to anti-theism.

Like other forms of utilitarian theory, flexitarianism is entirely irrational when considered as a pragmatic or scientific matter. It makes as much sense as partial opposition to rape, or occasional opposition to racism, and it's only because these things are against the law that flexitarianism isn't judged with the same intensity. If Singer were to suggest flexitarianism with respect to eating farmed humans (after all, he claims humans and animals are equal in suffering) one would assume the morally untenable position he advocates would be easier to oppose.

ALL ANIMAL ETHICS HELPS?

As someone who has been involved in animal ethics for many years, more of my time has been spent on explaining why that statement in the sub-title doesn't make sense than anything else. There is a mistaken assumption that as humans become kinder, everything gets better; thus all animal ethics is positive in net effect by pushing the interests of animals and thereby pushing us to be more empathetic. There is, as so often, intuitive appeal to this widely believed statement. Over time, as we have grown more rational, we have undoubtedly become kinder and less harsh with each other and so in turn, society is now a better place to live. Pinker argues this with the strongest analysis one would think is possible.[82] However as I stated earlier, and have argued throughout, this decrease in violence does not transfer to animals as they are not *in* society. Systems like welfarism allow us to use (and commit violence against) species of all kinds, whilst remaining largely removed from the process. Welfarism unintentionally therefore acts to justify and continue violence, in a sense. Our kindness, in wanting to exploit nonhumans in nicer ways, has led to nicer sounding animal products and a matching

---

[82] Pinker, 2011.

perception that we are indeed treating animals better. But it hasn't actually improved a great deal for animals due to economic barriers (namely welfarism), and has no cultural need to so long as the movement against animal use is stagnated by the variety of much easier options to appease guilt, like flexitarianism.

As such, my argument has made the point that not every form of animal ethics is helpful. Whilst we should consider speciesism to be a prejudice as bad as others like sexism or racism, this does not mean that animals are helped in the same way humans are. As we become kinder to each other, society is helped. But animals are outside of society; locked away in sheds and cages, or out of view under the sea. Our increasing rationality and kindness only helps them if we intentionally and rationally make it do so, and thus sceptically assess the problems with animal use *and* welfarism in the first place. At current all our kindness is doing is hiding the suffering away, making it more palatable for us humans to view, or making it seem 'better' than before, so in essence making it seem like progress is afoot and we need not worry.

The realisation that not all animal ethics helps is not limited to the understanding that welfarism is harmful, but also to more modern understandings of campaigns on behalf of animals. Kindness may help to mark a society who is more willing to help animals, but it doesn't currently entail one that is actually helping them. This is more rationally formed scepticism at work. It may seem a big step to have to consider veganism as a lifestyle change, but feel solace in the fact that the same argument which espouses rational veganism also promotes the opposition of the animal charities which most offend our cultural tastes: groups like PETA or VIVA!, with their bunny suits and anthropomorphic t-shirts.

SINGLE ISSUE CAMPAIGNS

Francione occasionally touches on the problems with single issue campaigns in his published work on welfarism, but never gets near enough to explicitly pointing out their problematic nature. Indeed in *Rain Without Thunder*[83] he makes an unnecessary distinction between 'abolitionist' and 'non-abolitionist' single issue campaigns. Non-abolitionist *single issue campaigns (SICs)* are those exemplifying the welfarist approach, which aim to regulate animal use (a campaign for free range eggs rather than battery eggs, for example), whilst abolitionist SICs are those with which one might campaign to abolish a particular animal use (a campaign to end all uses of animals for fur, for example).

Campaigns themselves are useful only as a pragmatic matter. They can help us get closer or further away from what the 'right thing' is. This is where welfarism falls down, but it's also where single issue campaigns as a whole fall down. A single issue campaign (of which welfare regulation is just one example) has many negative but necessary effects due to its very structure.

Firstly, it aims to differentiate between different types of animal use. It has to do this, as the aim of any single issue campaign (for example, to ban the use of wild animals in circuses) is to garner support for that one use without having to campaign for a much harder, more encompassing goal like veganism, or against animal entertainment as a whole. As such, the campaign aims to, and if it is successful it succeeds in, making this one animal use seem worse than others. As a tactical matter this involves the necessary implicit siding with the audience in agreeing all animal use isn't problematic, and then making the case for why this one on its own is problematic. Basically the campaigns indulge in a meaningful deception, for tactical purposes.

The SIC therefore can't use arguments based on the truth (like 'all animals deserve not to be imprisoned because they are sentient, and speciesism is irrational') and instead makes claims about one species, or the problems with our 'treatment' of animals in this one particular instance, or appeals to our basic emotional views by playing on subjective

[83] Rain Without Thunder: The Ideology of the Animal Rights Movement. Francione, G. L. 1996.

words like cruelty or compassion. This implicitly agrees that the problem isn't animal use, but rather the method of the use. And hence the SIC has the same effect as welfarism in pushing this idea that animals are our property to use in the first place. It suffers all the same problems that go with welfarism, even if it's better hidden in many SICs (opposing the social movement 'snowball', making people feel better about animal exploitation without doing anything significant: in this case because single issue campaigns rarely are successful, and when they are it is because the animal use in question was so rare in the first place).

One final point to take on board about single issue campaigns is 'low hanging fruit'. Often these campaigns are referred to like this, as the advocates see them as things we can do now, picking off the fruit from the animal exploitation tree one fruit at a time. As Dan Cudahy explains in his popular blog[84], the problems with this approach are many. First, there are infinite 'fruits' and whilst the advocates are spending huge amounts of resources picking off one, more will grow. After all, they are not advocating the reasons to not use animals, just the reasons not to use them in this one way. Secondly, this acts as 'pruning', allowing animal industry to remove extremely cruel looking practices to prune up the rest of the branch of exploitation (e.g., when using wild animals in circuses is opposed, it makes the use of domestic animals in circuses look humane and useful, and allows the growth there and elsewhere whilst attention is turned). Thirdly, every effort to hack at low fruit, or at low branches, is time that could be spent hacking at the roots. Speciesism is pervasive, and fighting it involves spreading the truth that speciesism is a prejudice and is immoral. The truth isn't going to surface with the welfarists' way of implicitly endorsing speciesism, or with the single issue campaigners' way of taking one fruit at a

---

[84] The argument is expanded upon wonderfully in Cudahy's collaboration with Angel Flinn in the essay for The Abolitionist entitled "Single Issue Campaigns: Pruning Exploitation" which can be found here:
http://www.theabolitionist.info/article/single-issue-campaigns-pruning-exploitation/

time (tactically engaging deceipt). Animal advocacy that consists of single issue campaigns is really nothing more than a collection of fabricated reasons why you should do what the advocate handing you the leaflet wants you to do. As a rationalist it is impossible to condone this as a method for advocating any moral cause: emotional or irrational appeals are the entire problem, not the solution, and people aren't going to drop prejudices this way.

Of course we need only look at the evidence in order to highlight the problems with single issue campaigns. The animal movement's most successful campaign of all time was the anti-fur campaign. Not only did they manage to make fur socially unacceptable, they also managed to ban its production on UK shores. Yet one brief look at recent news articles shows fur is coming back into fashion. What PETA and the other groups behind these campaigns had managed to do was to make fur socially unacceptable as a fashionable matter by using celebrity endorsements, descriptions of the overly 'cruel' treatment of animals on fur farms, etc. It wasn't 'cool' to wear fur, but PETA were cool. Now PETA have gotten old, and people grown tired of their wanting to ban not just fur but many types of animal uses under different, random emotional appeals, suddenly the 'coolness' factor has switched. PETA never attempted to foster a long term understanding with the problem of animal use, and instead campaigned on these immediately successful 'coolness' arguments. As a result, when the furore dies down, people go back to fur like anything else. The sales have hit new highs in recent years[85]. People never really understood PETA's arguments to be of rational value, because they weren't, so the anger faded as soon as the celebrity advertisements stopped: evidential proof that single issue campaigns are structurally flawed, by virtue of needing to differentiate

---

[85] http://www.guardian.co.uk/lifeandstyle/2009/nov/22/fur-rather-go-naked "In 2007, fur sales worldwide totalled £10bn, up 11% on the previous year, with nine years of continuous growth. Last year, the fur trade contributed £13bn to the global economy, and although fur farming was banned in Britain in 2003, the UK's fur trade turnover is about £400-500m a year."

themselves from the effective truth with use of emotive or narrow reasoning. I argued much earlier that we need to be careful with 'emotive' language for rational causes, and the supposed 'success' of the anti-fur campaigns that used it are perhaps the most prevalent warning. This is evidence which is relevant for any moral advocacy, and it asks us to strongly consider indulging rationality rather than short-term tactics.

THE IRRATIONALITY OF ANIMAL RIGHTS GROUPS

A worrying number of animal groups claim that violence and intimidation is a useful tool, or that veganism is about 'being compassionate', 'loving animals', or even that veganism is some ultimate marker of health or natural eating, on top of their attempts to justify welfarism and single issue campaigns in the face of solid reason. Thus it is little wonder that serious people don't take veganism for the serious obligation that it is. After all, current advocacy on veganism is almost entirely irrational.

This does not mean that veganism isn't to be taken seriously; for the same reason that if atheism had been the preserve of such poor arguments/tactics in history, it shouldn't be ignored on this basis either. It is, though, useful to separate these groups from veganism, as they do not stand up for the same rational veganism that I am advocating here. Over the last few years I've had wonderful support in my criticism of these types of animal rights groups, from a variety of intelligent and rationally valuing people across the world who are in complete agreement with what rational morality advocates. Unsurprisingly these kinds of vegans often also value the tenets of anti-theism and rational consistency. Yet these are the precious few and are far outweighed by a vocal majority ignoring any sort of reason-based analysis.

The spiritual ideas put across by animals groups, often focusing on ideas we can generously call 'compassion', manifest themselves even in the best current animal rights theory available. Aforementioned scholar Gary L. Francione, who pioneered most aspects of the abolitionist critique of animal advocacy, is perhaps the best example of this. He states that his theory is not scientifically provable, but rather rests upon 'the truth of non-violence'[86]. Indeed, one wonders why those ideas like welfarism (which he rightly shows to be counter-productive) cannot be justified by the claim that they rest on the 'truth of welfare regulation', if we are going to accept that random spiritual ideas can be valid assumptions. Indeed, given the inability to defend welfarism, yet the fervent way groups like PETA indulge in it, this very well may be argued to be their position.

In any case, Francione's assumptions (which rest on spiritual ideas) are part and parcel of the reason why people are simply not flocking to veganism, and why vegans themselves are not flocking to 'abolitionism' (which is the position Francione names his own). It even explains why most people don't bother with morality at all. Literally everyone in society believes that faith is an okay way to form beliefs. Indeed, Francione and the rest of the animal movement appear to embrace this with open arms, happy to argue at a level of immaterial, personal 'truth' which is no better than religious wars that are started over whose God is right on some random issue.

To his credit, Francione rises above much of this arguing from a spiritual basis, by making many of his arguments (like the anti-welfarism arguments, as previously explained) of a rational and evidence based variety. However, can he really expect many of those who are supportive of welfarism to drop their own 'personal truths' and embrace his rational arguments, when his own position (which uses rationality) is based on 'personal truths' in the first place? So long as the 'truth of non-violence' is all that's holding up his ideas, it's no better than showing Muslims the rationale behind why there is no 'Allah' and expecting them to then start believing in a Christian God. The analogy isn't perfect, and of course some people will still see the problems with welfarism due to

---

[86] http://www.abolitionistapproach.com/new-atheism-and-animal-ethics-some-reflections/

Francione's tireless efforts to promote abolitionism, but it's doubtful that such a method will set the world on fire. The fact that 20 years of abolitionist theory has created nothing but a small pocket of abolitionists in each country, while most animal rights people flock to single issue campaigners like PETA, is perhaps telling.

CONSERVATIONISM: IT ISN'T ABOUT ANIMALS

At the start of this chapter I briefly alluded to conservationism as an often mistaken choice. This is incorrect in some respects. Conservation of the environment, of green space and of natural animal habitats is entirely necessary, and even morally obligatory. We shouldn't be arrogantly dumping waste around, just as we shouldn't be using resources we don't need in a world where resources may soon be worryingly thin on the ground.

However the type of animal conservationism mentioned (the type done by the WWF and others) is rather irrational. These groups focus not on the interests of individual sentients, but rather on the interests of biological categories. For instance, the WWF are not concerned with the suffering an individual might feel, but rather with the depletion of a category of animal (a species).

We should treat this claim with extreme caution. A depleting species can be an entirely natural and necessary occurrence. We shouldn't destroy the habitats of sentient individuals, but we also shouldn't be overly concerned about individuals who are naturally dying out simply because they are at an evolutionary dead end (perhaps like Pandas, with their disastrously low sex drive and reliance on nutritionally sparse bamboo) so to speak. Yet these groups aim specifically at these species, intending to garner empathy for a biological category rather than the experiencing individuals themselves. This is human empathy getting carried away with itself to a vastly irrational place of no good. Pandas are arguably not better off in zoos, and if they die out whilst we are leaving their habitat alone to give them a chance to live, then what is the problem with this extinction?

Take the more radical conservationist and media friendly Sea Shepherd group. They spend millions upon millions rescuing a few whales every year[87], whilst trillions die in human exploitation of other animals, and whilst many members of the crew of the Sea Shepherd aren't even vegans once they go back to their everyday lives (and so arguably indulge in more needless exploitation than they stop). It is peculiar. The WWF thrives on our earlier mentioned unfortunate inability to differentiate the plight of one individual from the more important plight of many, whilst the Sea Shepherd thrives on the donations of rebellious, drama and 'direct-action' loving animal advocates. This is simply not charity, in the same way that wearing a white lab coat doesn't make someone a dentist. The rational-moral of the story? You wouldn't pay people to fix your teeth just because they wear white coats, so don't support people in the name of charity just because they claim to be activists.

In all seriousness, we should be concerned that our morality is becoming tied up in category orientated, misanthropic ethics rather than rationally asserted, practical theory. If *rational veganism* is an area of ethics that my theory can create/jump on board with, conservationism of this type is one it wholeheartedly opposes. As I stated earlier, we need to be very wary of mainstream charities and movements of all types. All animal ethics certainly doesn't help just by virtue of its intention.

While it is irrational to put animals on an intellectual or spiritual pedestal, it is also irrational for us to assert that we can use them as our property in the first place. We have no explicit need to use animals for food, clothing or the variety of other uses we find for them, so justifying this immense level of suffering and death is not logically sound. I only see one topic — vivisection — where we can justify our use of animals

---

[87] http://www.theage.com.au/national/how-sea-shepherd-stays-afloat-20120110-1ptu6.html

in anything but frivolous terms. I cannot find moral logic to support the sacrifice of millions of animals for gradual scientific improvement (it is not even a moral case of one animal life in exchange for one human life, as many propose), and I hope that sooner rather than later we can completely replace the remaining numbers of animals in our research. However, even if we conceded a necessity for vivisection, we would still face recognition that 99.9% of the billions of animals we kill each year happen to be completely unnecessary and irrational. This might be the biggest single aspect of switching to a rational morality.

7. Determinism and Free Will

In accepting rationality as the basic guide for our behaviour, and accepting morality as a rational, scientific endeavour, there is one big area that stands out (second only to atheism and animal ethics, in my mind). That area is determinism and the notion that free will, in the sense that we generally think of it, doesn't actually exist. Like almost every other area of this book, if you aren't familiar with determinism then this isn't going to sit well with your initial intuitions. Indeed, the counterintuitive initial nature of determinism is one that proves, again, just how fallible even the most seemingly secure of our intuitions are in the face of reason.

However, it has been known for a while now that we live in a world of cause and effect. Science is able to make marvellous advances and technological leaps, and all of this is due to the deterministic nature of the world. If things happened randomly, then science would be at a loss. If when trying to decode the human genome similar results were different every day, then we wouldn't have gotten far. Similarly, in the world the rest of us inhabit, if we were trying to build a road, and for no reason the consistency of the tarmac varied so as to be unpredictable on a random basis, we couldn't even begin to lay it. Science works in a large part because we can make predictions about anything, based on the fact that it only reacts given certain factors, and not randomly. Causation is as provable as provable can get.

This is not to say we don't occasionally describe something as random because we don't know how it works, and might never be able to know, but randomness itself is a mythical quality designed to explain this exact human limit of not being able to know. Indeed, randomness, like God, is an explanation often utilised when we don't know why something happens. But as a scientific matter, there is no reason to suppose that randomness exists at all. As we will see later, certain areas of science challenge this but do not prove randomness exists.

131

FREE WILL

Humans (and other animals, for that matter) are not just objects, but organic life forms that have evolved certain conscious capabilities. We feel pain and can make decisions in real time based on our experiences. We can also act in real time with our experiences (milliseconds after coming across stimuli) and so can utilise our sentient capabilities to our great benefit; giving us, as animals, a huge advantage over individual plants and other non-conscious organisms in continuing to survive. Imagine us, if you will, as plants that grew the ability to react and run away, or fight others who wanted to eat us[88]. We're much more likely to survive than plants that are rooted to the spot and which can only react gradually to stimuli like sunlight.

This inherent advantage, consciousness, has been philosophised to be many things over the ages (a link to God, a gift of stewardship to the Earth, etc.[89]). One of those which most societies believe in is that coupled with rationality, consciousness gives us free will. This is the idea that although we were once other individuals, and once other organisms, with consciousness and rationality came the ability to choose our fate like never before. We have an ability to choose what happens to us, rise above our instincts and live in the world as free agents. Unlike plants, which are guided by basic stimuli, and animals, who are guided by their instincts.

There is much to be said for the way consciousness/sentience sets us apart from other organisms, certainly, and indeed I've so far argued that conscious individuals are the only recipients of morality. However, determinism categorically shows that free will doesn't exist in the slightest. This is counterintuitive as we feel like we have free will. I look at a dog salivating at food, or a gerbil compelled to chew cardboard I give to her, and I feel ruled by my instincts to a

---

[88] I am not making the claim that we were ever plants, in our evolutionary history, though we might have been plants of some sorts at some point.

[89] Consciousness itself seems to be at the heart of most Abrahamic religion, for instance, with our current and historical inability to theorise what exactly consciousness entails leading to all manner of predictable religious charlatans exploiting this lack of understanding.

lesser degree than those two animals are. I believe that because I have a capacity for explicit rationality, my consciousness is of a type through which my choices are not chosen and guided by instinct, but rather chosen by me, as a person who is examining their environment.

Yet determinism shows that no matter how free we feel, we are still recipients of a rich history of experiences, going all the way back to that time when our parents conceived us. Starting at the beginning, we came into existence as the result of two merging cells (an event not chosen or willed by us in any way, as cells themselves hold no consciousness, never mind rationality) and from that moment on, what happened to us was also not our choice. We didn't choose how our mother carried us in her womb, or where to, and likely the first influence we had on anyone else, as conscious individuals, was instinctually formed when living in the womb: perhaps a kick here or a turn there, which may have influenced our mother's behaviour or the behaviours of other noticing parties. Even if we assume that from that moment of initial, instinctual consciousness that eventually resulted in a movement, we were 'choosing' what happened, we still have never had free will as that movement *itself* was the result of two cells being formed weeks before we had these conscious instincts, and there have been millions of cellular and environmental happenings since then that we weren't the conscious authors of. As such, there was never a time when we began by making a decision; we have always been agents acting from experiences and genetic occurrences which we didn't choose.

From this simple fact we can draw out cause and effect. You kicked not because you randomly or spiritually decided to kick, but because something compelled you to kick; or screamed when you were born not because you randomly or spiritually wanted to scream, but because something compelled you to scream. Cause and effect means that you were never an agent acting free of your genes and experiences, and if you join the dots from any action in your life, you can draw right back to it being the fault of two cells merging, which is in turn the fault of other activities (in this case, an activity by your parents which you probably don't want to think about). No decision you make is truly 'free'.

This has interesting connotations. At every point in your life, in every single nanosecond, every thought going through your head and every decision you intentionally make is the result not of a truly free choice, but rather is predetermined to happen. You think you are making a choice between two different options, but realistically you are choosing no more than the dog is choosing to salivate, the gerbil is choosing to chew the cardboard, or the plant is choosing to bloom. Had every factor been the same (all genetic and worldly experiences had happened in exactly the same way, all thoughts were exactly the same, etc.) you couldn't have chosen to do otherwise at any point. This is no less true for the plant, the gerbil or the dog than it is for you.

Scientific evidence has also begun to support this kind of reason. Libet, et al, in an influential 1983 study, conducted an experiment to discover if cerebral activity could be recorded before we make a decision, to note whether the action is really well on its way to happening before we are aware of it[90]. They categorically discovered that "The onset of cerebral activity clearly preceded by at least several hundred milliseconds the reported time of conscious intention to act." The findings of this study are doubted by some, including those who note that perhaps this shows that the brain is 'aware' and ready to make a decision, not necessarily already deciding before we consciously know. Perhaps they are right. But however we make sense of the results, there is definitely brain activity there which we are not aware of, which is doing work before we consciously decide on an act. Thus, whichever way one looks at it, we are not the conscious authors of all that happens in our brain. Add this to our knowledge of cause and effect, and there's only one conclusion to draw.

---

[90] Time of conscious intention to act in relation to onset of cerebral activity (readiness-potential). The unconscious initiation of a freely voluntary act. Libet B, Gleason CA, Wright EW, Pearl DK. 1983. Brain: A Journal of Neurology.

Moral implications

Our lack of free will doesn't mean that we should never punish someone for their actions. Rational morality, as I have explained it, is just that-rational. Allowing a serial killer to walk the streets just because he isn't to blame in a philosophical account of free will is not rational. Sure, we should not punish someone for punishment's sake. This means that if we see no benefit to punishment, in that there is no safety increase for society, no rehabilitative possibility from the punishment, and no far reaching societal effect in providing a detrimental situation for acting in the immoral way, then the punishment should not be administered. However, it is hard to see how this will impact on most of societal punishment anyway, which is primarily conducted for the above purposes. Punishment is rational even though we might not be to blame for the action which is being punished.

We should bear it in mind for the minority situations in which criminals are locked up for no reason. However, as earlier stated, allowing for individual cases like this to have an effect on general societal rules isn't very practical and might well result in laws being gotten around. So in effect, determinism and our lack of free will may be a subject which is practically null in legal terms. We should take it on board, if individual situations allow without sacrificing a wider ranging rational analysis, but this might not ever even occur.

As a more relevant point, we should be aware of the truth about free will on an individual level. People aren't intrinsically evil, but rather are recipients of the deterministic nature of the universe. As much as people may be to blame for committing an act at a societal level, they are not so much to blame as individuals–but rather we all are responsible as a society. It's our society that has made these persons the way they are, and it is in our interactions with them and others that we can avoid their becoming obstacles to civilised people. Understanding the nature of determinism, and our lack of free will, allows us to truly see how practical ethics works; how we are all players in a society grander than our own individual organisms – a society which creates the problems it is trying to get rid of. Understanding our role in creating these problems, and the rational nature of being generally 'nicer' or more respectful perhaps, is something vital to any successful moral code. Society should be taught that we need to punish people; however it isn't anger, but sympathy that should be going the way of the punished party. Punishment is a useful concept unless we reach a state where people are all rational machines, but it is not a philosophically sound result of analysing 'fault'.

But science shows 'cause and effect' is not the whole story, doesn't it?

It seems that whenever a rational idea is disliked on personal grounds, ideas like quantum theory are wheeled out, caked in misapprehension and relieved of central limbs, to back up the opposition. Just as I'm sure that critics will point to fictional, media labelled 'perfect rationalists' like Dr. House, MD, or any cold yet brilliant detective in order to argue that rationality does not cause kindness, I'm sure that they will mutilate quantum theory and then show its half-dismembered carcass as a reason why determinism doesn't exist, and why we all have free will.

The argument will go that science has uncovered activity at particle level which does not appear to act in a 'cause and effect' manner, and thus the universe, which is made up of an innumerable number of particles, is not based on 'cause and effect', either.

To be honest, even if particle physics did turn out to be an area in which randomness does exist, it wouldn't say anything about determinism. We can carry out an infinite number of experiments on humans to show that they are influenced by the world around them and are created by genes, and given that we know thoughts don't appear at random we can be fairly certain that determinism exists. So even if sub atomic particles appear to act randomly, they are obviously not affecting our actions as larger entities in any meaningful way as *we* don't appear to act randomly. Indeed, no area of science appears to act randomly, and everything is made of supposedly random sub atomic particles. At worst, this shows that the sub-atomic world is not disintegrating our physical laws at societal level, and so is not affecting our deterministic natural universe. But more likely is that this level of science (which exists at base level in everything) is simply not yet understood properly. It would be odd that our building blocks were not somehow explainable, and various physicists around the world are working on ironing out this interesting problem as I type.

This is the second relevant point that the criticism always misses: particle activity isn't necessarily random just because it appears random in some aspects. Throughout history science has continually solved seemingly paradoxical instances and has many times turned the 'assumed random' into the 'rationally caused'. Particle physics seems like a whole different kettle of artichokes, however, given that which sub-atomic particles make up (larger objects) do act in a cause and effect way, and given that what we know about science couldn't have been established without the law of cause and effect, which in turn would mean billions of observations and results couldn't have been explained by following these laws, then it is irrational to claim the world is 'random' and that things aren't working on a cause and effect basis. You don't burn down the kitchen, move out of your house and head into space on a rocket to find a new universe to inhabit just because your dish rag is dirty. Similarly, you don't dump thousands of years of truth finding because of one area seeming anomalous. Perhaps particle physics is anomalous, or perhaps we just don't understand yet how it isn't. Either way, we are very likely to uncover better ways to answer these questions.

DOES DETERMINISM MEAN WE SHOULDN'T BOTHER?

Many people believe that if determinism is true, then why bother at all? Indeed, if we can never truly choose otherwise, why choose at all? What we do is already determined to happen.

This kind of problem comes up in two ways. Firstly, fatalism: the idea that if we are already determined, there is nothing we can do to change our fate, so we shouldn't bother. This is a logical fallacy. Determinism explains how if things were to happen in exactly the same way again, they couldn't happen differently and you couldn't choose differently. It does not mean we do not have a choice at the social level, it just means we couldn't have chosen differently, had things been the same again.

This doesn't mean that we should just stop, as everything is already decided. Nothing is decided, and there is no great plan. Indeed, even if we were in a state of perfect technology and understanding, and could figure out what the future would look like starting from now, it would already be different to what we have theorised as our very understanding of it changes its result. We are determined to act in certain ways as a result of previous events, yes, but we are not fated to act in a certain way so that certain events couldn't change some determined fate. There is a slight, but distinct difference.

The second result of this argument is not so much fatalism as excusitarianism, if I may invent such a concept. This is not that we are fated to act a certain way, but rather that we couldn't act any other way, so why bother doing anything nice/stressful/hard. Essentially it is misunderstanding what determinism means. If you are acting like a twit, you probably couldn't have acted like anything but a twit if the same set of circumstances were to happen again. However, going forwards, you may or may not act like a twit depending on what you choose to do. You are still free to choose to act like a twit, or to refrain, it's just that your genes and experiences are the reason for the choice rather than your immortal soul or evil nature. The kinds of free will excusitarianism pretends doesn't exist, actually still do: not in a non-deterministic sort of way, but we still effect the world by acting, thus excusitarianism is just a misunderstanding.

Excusitarianism makes little sense. It is essentially a pragmatic theory, trying to excuse one's actions by reference to the fact you couldn't have chosen to do otherwise. But excuses are fairly unimportant when the punishment for societally immoral actions is not given based on 'fault'. So long as the punishment itself is based on the consequential basis for the punishment (like security, rehabilitation or deterrence), rather than on some notion of punishing just because it's a person's fault, then the excusitarian position is illogical. There's no benefit to being an excusitarian, just as there is no logical reason to be one. Yes we are creatures of cause and effect, but that doesn't mean that our actions don't still have an effect on ourselves and others. You couldn't have chosen to do otherwise, but it's still important that you choose one way and not the other most of the time. Moreover, you can still be punished for acting immorally, so excusitarianism is fruitless.

FREE WILL AS A DELUSION OF RATIONALITY

Just as religious and spiritual belief can be shown to be a delusion of rationality (a desire to find truth in the face of unanswered questions) so can the belief of free will. People don't like what a world without free will would look like, and that lack of affection comes from a similar misunderstanding as the religious desire to argue against atheism.

Spiritualism argues against determinism, as it doesn't like the idea that there is no god pulling the strings, or no spiritual sphere we can float away in. Alternatively, Fatalism and Excusitarianism are positions which oppose free will because they don't like what they think it entails: concerns which are comforted by analysis of the facts and dissolving of the myths.

As I have argued throughout, we make our decisions and form our positions rationally, and on determinism that is no different. As important as it is to understand why determinism is true, and why we don't hold a classical notion of free will, it is also important to understand why people choose any of the excuses or positions against it. They do so as they believe it rational in order to continue either their perceived rationally formed moral codes (like in the case of religion/spirituality, where they feel morality is rational, but can only fathom the spiritual reasons for it, so want to twist things like determinism that disprove spiritual ideas) or perceived rational reasons for acting (in the case of Fatalism and Excusitarianism, whose proponents genuinely believe determinism to be illogical in disallowing them to act in the way that they feel they can).

It's important to undertake this exercise at any stage in a rational theory of morality, as it allows us to see how people are making decisions rationally, and so are valuing rationality at every point, and moreover so we can see that the problem is a lack of rational consistency rather than there being no reason to value rationality in the first place. The oppositions to determinism are rationally formed, but lacking the evidence or intention to rationally understand.

THE PRO-SOCIAL BENEFITS OF FEELING FREE?

There is a famous study (by no means the only one on this subject) authored by Baumeister et al.[91], which claims that a belief in free will may *"foster a sense of thoughtful reflection and willingness to exert energy, thereby promoting helpfulness and reducing aggression, and so disbelief in free will may make behavior more reliant on selfish, automatic impulses and therefore less socially desirable."* Indeed, there are a number of studies which claim to show similar results. Does this mean that it is rational to pragmatically trick people into believing they have free will?

Firstly, as specified a number of times, if morality is to be considered science it can't very well fudge results. We can feel at liberty to have societies where punishments occur, but we're also rationally obliged to tell people this is the case not because people are to blame, but because we need to protect one another. Tricking people into believing irrational ideas, as a tool for keeping people nice and helpful, is decidedly irrational. Sure, rational morality appears to have pragmatic benefits in every area, but at the same time the scientific aspect should always outweigh the pragmatic. This comes

---

[91] http://psp.sagepub.com/content/35/2/260.short

from a scientific understanding: we don't fly to the moon sitting on banana skins because it is scientifically impossible. Whilst moral science doesn't make it physically impossible to act in immoral ways, it does make it morally impossible. So while it may be scientifically possible to deceive people en masse, for political reasons, it is not morally rational in the way I've argued that rational morality must be. Put simply, physical science defines what we physically can and cannot do. Moral science defines what we should and should not do. Rather than pragmatically fudging results in either, we are obligated to be rational.

Secondly, as a practical matter, the reason the earlier mentioned experiments get the results they do is precisely because of the myths about determinism; myths I have so far debunked, which manifest in the four spheres of Religious, Spiritual, Fatalism and Excusitarianism. The latter two are the kinds of behaviour which experiments seem to show exist in belief in determinism, but the experiments themselves are flawed precisely because they do not explain, and more importantly foster an understanding, that determinism does not imply Fatalism and Excusitarianism. People intuitively believe determinism does imply fatalism, upon hearing that free will doesn't exist, and these ideas need rational analysis to be debunked. Rational analysis results in rational understanding; something which is not allowed for in the method or the timespan of these experiments. Were the experiments to explain the reasons why determinism doesn't mean fatalism, and why it doesn't allow for excusitarianism either, and the participants were able to come to terms with what it rationally does involve in due time, one can be sure the findings would be different. Indeed, experiments in which anyone's basic moral beliefs were shown to be false would be likely to result in the findings that these experiments on determinism show, so allowing time to adjust to the rational truth that morality still exists would be the key to avoiding the problems.

As a final point, would it even be creating a morally able society if we deceived people into acting in a good way by invoking ideas like free will or any other mythical concepts? It might, at least in the short term. However, as with the problems of a society that believes in religion (and the faith-based problems that go with) making people act in a nice way through deception is not really what we want, is it? Don't we want people to understand the world, strive to know more about it and act nicely because they truly believe it is the rational and honest thing to do? The way to this world is by enlightening people with reality, not treating them like they can't handle the truth.

CONCLUSION

As a parting point to remember: we still live, we still feel, we are still conscious and morality is still rational. We simply have to admit that our lives happen on top of scientific laws, not outside of them. Free will doesn't add meaning, and if we don't act well we will be determined to irrational, immoral lives, just as if we do act well we will be determined to more rational, moral lives. Determinism doesn't change this; it just helps to see that we are all responsible, to some degree, for each other as well as ourselves. This rational fact fundamentally changes the way we should view morality.

We don't know what we are determined to do, and everything we learn and act out changes our future significantly just like it did prior to accepting determinism. The difference is that we are discovering our futures as agents consisting of only genes and experiences, rather than as spiritually immaterial, blame and praise worthy souls.

8. Liberal Politics and Movements

It was touched on upon the formulation of rational morality that prejudice is not at all rational. From this it was probably clear that the political significance of this theory is not minor. Just as we can show general prejudice to be irrational, of course looking after the self is still particularly rational because you are as good a sentient being as any other. As such the aspect of the role rational morality plays in politics has to be examined; differing political positions push different moral perspectives, so if morality can be considered a science then these political positions hold truth values. We can look for evidence to show the problems with any given position and remove the idea that most of the differences in political opinion (at least those related to morality) are based on personal taste.

My analysis of the practical side of rational morality is, as throughout, nothing more than an introduction to these topics. Never is this truer than with a discussion of politics, as the area is so complex and varied that to define such clear answers as one might come to in animal ethics or determinism, for example, is impossible. Hence my comments on politics might seem vague. Although these are largely intentional general comments, this should not take away from the fact that analysis should still be rationally and evidence based. Had I already formulated a perfectly rational political way forward, you can be sure that this book would have been preceded by it, but this doesn't mean we can't still make informed, rational (though potentially not completely perfect) decisions in the area of politics.

POLITICAL THEORIES – A BASIC POSITION

In providing a new theory of morality, I don't believe it is my job to push certain political positions, or rubbish others, but what should be clear after the following few paragraphs is that there are political positions which are morally irrational, just as surely as there are positions that are better.

If we look to where an anti-prejudice stance might start, most will immediately look to Karl Marx[92]. Marx's longstanding critique of capital and the role of capitalism as exploitative in society is an influential one and appears to have rational roots. Simply put, if nothing else, we can take from him the idea that it is wrong for us to get caught up in improving things as an industrial matter when net impact is negative on groups of individual people. For the purposes of being clear and rationally consistent with what we now know morality entails, we can also replace 'people' with 'sentient individuals'. It is irrational to further industrial capacity, to increase the coffers of a small minority or a system (like a business), whilst individuals elsewhere suffer with not enough resources to go around. This doesn't flaw all capitalism any more than it supports all protest of it; however as a general rule it is something to be aware of.

From here, one might also suggest anarchism as having a useful goal. Anarchism in its purest form outright rejects prejudice, capitalism and authority, replacing them with the idea that if we are morally educated (in this case, morally rational), then we don't need 'controlling' and society itself will be more civilised. People shouldn't be governed for governance sake, and liberal rights of individuals should be respected as far as possible. There are advantages to an anarchist position; I mean who would seriously object to anarchism being a utopian ideal? A world with no hierarchy automatically battles prejudice and equality is formed necessarily. However, it is the practical possibility that critiques it.

One of the things I am arguing in this book is that as people become more rationally intentioned, and more explicitly rational in their decisions, they will both be discovering truth and arguably become better people toward each other. However, I have also warned of the evidence that

---

[92] *Das Kapital.* Marx, K. 1867.

shows we are not ever going to be perfect, rational machines. In chapter 6 I discussed that the only rational option with regards to animal ethics is anti-speciesism, and hopefully progressing toward an eventual abolition of industrial animal use, however I don't envisage that one day all animal exploitation will disappear, just as I don't envisage that all human violence will disappear. Yet a positing of anarchism as a practical notion, rather than a utopian ideal, requires this desire for total abolition of exploitation to be true, or at least to be true to a degree where we no longer require any authority interference.

Whilst it seems plausible to state that adopting an anarchic state might be possible one day, and harbour better results than society at the moment, there doesn't seem to be any evidence that it will ever be better than having a reduced, non-controlling authority based on equality laws. Indeed, if equality laws were properly upheld there's every reason to suppose that to be a realistic solution. However, the effect of anarchism not just on functioning, normal members of human societies, but also on nonhuman animals, must be taken into account. In legal processes, we can hope to one day get to a stage where nonhumans are protected with a law of 'a right not to be used as property' or something similar. It is unclear how nonhumans could be protected and looked out for so well without some form of authority, given their inability to speak or participate in society. They are often ignored in theories which preach for non-authority, and will naturally become the most likely victims along with the perceivably weaker (the young and the infirm) members of the human race: victims of rationally capable individuals who are not ever going to be perfectly rational, and so are likely to need rules and codes from agreed, collective authority of some degree. This, at least, is my opinion.

Anyway, I confess immediately that such discussion is currently conjectured. We have no evidence that anarchism works. However, we also have no evidence that it doesn't, given that states of solid, moral education and peaceful co-operation among humans, as well as moral respect for nonhumans, would be required before anarchism could even be thought about. We do, however, have evidence that prejudice is wrong, and that the Marxist critique of capitalism is partly rationally founded by relation to the theory I have so far put forth. As such, it makes sense that in a capitalist society (in which most of us currently live), there will be political positions currently being populated which are irrational in a very real sense.

CONSERVATISM AND THE FOCUS ON MONEY

At least here in the UK, Conservatism might be the most popular form of irrational politics available. The Conservative party were elected into government in the UK at the 2010 general election (via forming the largest part of a coalition) and ran their campaigns on several points that may be considered as appealing to our irrational prejudice and societal faiths, rather than to any good, solid development of society. We saw campaigns based around immigration, money, country isolation (in the forms of anti-European connections that are not explicitly money-based) and tax advantages. Rather than focus on the problems of these campaigns, one can note that these campaigns reflect societal opinion. Politicians in democratic society play the role of representing us, and Conservatism has developed from its racist, elitist roots to attempt to appear as 'middle ground' in order to gain election, in the same way the Labour Party have shifted from their leftist, trade union roots in order to do the same thing. So what must be clear, before politics is discussed at all, is that the problems are with us and not being manu-factured by some evildoers in historic London buildings. Politicians certainly aren't helping, but they are only as much to blame as each of us. We live in a deterministic world, remember, a world where governments are *caused* by our opinions and voting patterns.[93] Were we to change those, government would necessarily change too.

Money and 'Things'

A real, rational take on morality, means a real, rational re-examination of our views in core areas. As such the first area of interest is fairly obvious, as explained by the ideas of Marx: money and 'things' aren't everything.

Right now most of us live in a capitalist system (for better or worse) and so we can't underestimate the importance of money. It makes the world go round, as they say. But we only need enough for security. It's almost impossible to change these kinds of views overnight, and it would be decidedly irrational to give away all of our belongings in the name of charity or in some spiritual act of God. However we do need to look in the mirror and ask if we really need the money and 'things' that we have; or rather more importantly, whether we need hoards more of them.

No one wants to write clichés, just as no one wants to state the obvious, but most human beings in the world live in poverty. One can ignore this as the fact they already knew and forget about it tomorrow morning, or one can change their view slightly. I'm not advocating a zero-consumer society, neither am I advocating any form of returning to wilderness. These are actions which also would be decidedly irrational, and consist of generalist martyrdom and misplaced affection for the past, respectively. But we do need to start doing something meaningful, such as rejecting politicians' promises that we'll make more money from our earnings this

---

[93] Since writing this it has been bought to my attention that my theory may be overly simplistic in not noting the powerful interests that politicians often represent. I fully concur that the level of influence that business has in government reaches worrying levels in many democracies. However, those businesses are still run by people. We can judge systems to our hearts' content, but behind these systems are people. Similarly, behind a democratic government is a population of people voting for them. In the UK, for instance, if we wanted to opt for a political party with less business influence, we could happily choose any of the main parties other than the Conservatives (who receive more party funding from business than any other main party). We choose not to. And hence our support keeps allowing these people to make the decisions.

year via tax breaks, instead daring to plump for the options which actually increase taxes for those of us who are relatively well off, while decreasing them for the poorer, and supporting issues like effective forms of foreign aid. There are no simple rules when it comes to materialism, but there is a simple rule when it comes to morality: *be rational*, and that involves a profound sense of honesty and discarding our selfishness. The kind of view that we should do what is best for the world, rather than trying to justify our selfish opinions as being acceptable, is not beyond any of us. A world where the majority held and acted upon this view would be a much better world for everyone to live in.

Immigration

I won't attempt to explain why we need to lessen our strong, reactive views about immigration until I've briefly explained some rational ideas, which we could all do well to remember. Human beings were not created by God, or Allah, or any other deity, and just as surely as the world didn't start the day you were born, it also didn't start the day human beings first meaningfully existed. We evolved from the same ancestors as modern apes; indeed, we are still primates ourselves. Not only do the separate species of humans and other apes share a common ancestor (a time when we were both back as genes inside the same individual) but all humans also share a much more recent group of common ancestors. As far as evidence shows, all humans come from the same evolutionary ancestors in Africa, who themselves evolved from other apes. And even if we don't believe this (which the majority of scientists do), other evidence shows that human beings are almost exactly the same at genetic level–making our 96% genetic similarity to chimps look insignificant.

This short history/biology lesson has relevance. It shows that categories such as 'British', 'English', 'Scottish', 'American', 'German' or 'Ethiopian' are human constructs, simply describing where a person lives or was born. Modern day immigration rules and codes across the world, partly formed by religious conventions and disagreements, paint the world to be a place where humans have further evolved drastically into nations of separate and distinct people. Whereas the truth is that these borders and boundaries are as irrational as anything one could describe. They are useful purely as a pragmatic matter in helping to form societies (by helping calculate necessary services and tax distribution), but in no way should one take them as 'rights' to live in or visit certain places. *We are all Africans*, as the famous slogan says, and it couldn't be a truer statement.

Dawkins approaches this problem in an essay on the discontinuous mind in the 2011 Christmas edition of the New Statesman magazine.[94] As humans we are desperate to categorise and box things, and Dawkins states we should cross out boxes on forms which ask for our nationality or race and write instead 'human'. Whilst this would cause all manner of administrative issues for health care provisions or emergency response teams, Dawkins has a point. There is no reason to suggest we should not be allowed to enter other countries based on where we were born, or who our parents were, and so long as people are respectful of us, we should have no right to demand they not live next to us or visit the countries we currently inhabit. Such views on immigration are not just intellectually ignorant by the rigours of rational morality, they are also already identified as such by many individuals in society.

The sorts of battles that take place on immigration in the legal arena cloak themselves in a much more respectful tone than the racist ideas that I imply and disagree with in the above paragraph. Politicians talk of protecting services, respecting the role immigration plays in our societies, limiting it, and safeguarding (insert random nationality to describe any number of countries' political debates) 'British' jobs. But the essence is the same. Even if there were a problem with immigration 'stealing' 'British' jobs, one might ask why a

---

[94] The Tyranny of the Discontinuous Mind. P 54-57.

British person has a right to work in the UK, but a French person doesn't, simply because the British person was 'here longer'. Shouldn't the reasoning go that the person who is best at the job gets it, not the person with the right nationality? And even if we find rational reason to protect 'British' jobs, why is such a relatively small problem (dealing as it does with hundred thousands of people who can be labelled as immigrants, which cannot relate to more than fifty thousands of narrowly defined 'British' people losing jobs) getting the press reaction of millions of people? Clearly the proportions are out, and this signals the intention is not fairness, but rather an underlying xenophobia at least; perhaps one that is intensified by the media. We need a good study of moral science on the issue of immigration.

THE ENVIRONMENT

In almost every piece of writing I do, I steer clear of environmental issues simply as the message is automatically incorporated in other things I say. For example, if we genuinely and rationally respect each other (regardless of race or species, etc.) then one simply can't be too greedy, use too many resources, or wreck the environment for others. Respecting the environment is essentially an automatic by-product of being rational, so there is little reason to mention it. I also don't think I've ever met a person who believes there is no reason to worry about the environment–not honestly, or recently, anyway. Perhaps I simply don't go out of my way to talk to oddballs: I've also yet to meet any current member of the Westboro Baptist Church. I believe that a person who is honest and rational about morality will have no need to be preached to on such issues (as they are so widely known about already), so I focus on advocating honesty and rationality instead.

However, given that this section regards the brief specifics of politics, environmental issues are worth noting. Climate change is no more scientifically doubted than evolution. The evidence is there for all to see and, despite the best efforts of hired academic jesters aiming to either make a reputation or a fortune for themselves, it has not been rationally hidden in any way. The failure of politicians to recognise the severity of a problem which threatens the life of every single person and animal on the planet is telling of a society that hasn't really grasped what is going on, or a society that doesn't understand or respect science. Or perhaps the problem is just a media that doesn't function properly with presenting evidence. Either way it's a worry.

The problem of climate change is reaching a catastrophic point of no return and the only genuine question is how soon that will happen. The rational thing to do is not to pretend that it isn't happening and thereby argue against it by searching out random bad science as one's proof. Neither is it rational to wait until someone makes us act before we're willing to change. Doing what we can to help now is the key. And as significant as collective small changes like recycling might be, the political and industrial arenas are the best bets. Political parties not appearing to do much of anything need to be ignored immediately to push this point home, and those promising the most progress – whether it involves higher taxes or not – need to be supported. It might sound simple, but often the most rational decisions are. It takes a complex structure of lies and ignorance to avoid rationality in most cases, and that is what we are faced with dissolving. Simplicity, so to speak, is on our side.

RELIGION AND POLITICS

Whilst it is a decreasing problem in increasingly secular societies, what should most fundamentally be clear to anyone who has read this theory so far, is that religion in politics should be opposed. Perhaps most prevalent and well known in US politics, religion plays a role on both the right and the left, and even in decidedly more secular Britain we see regular bowing to its magical powers and insistence on its wholesome effect.[95]

This is problematic on a very basic level, which any thinking person should be outraged about. Just as I didn't spend long respecting the ideas of 'imaginary friends', politics most certainly shouldn't bow to it either. Politics is about real people, their interests, and the far reaching effects on sentient individuals of all types. Allowing religion into this and talking of 'Christian morality' is akin to letting our interests play second fiddle to what a dusty, out of date fictional book says we should do. It's absurd.

As I have examined so far, religion is both irrational and encourages apathy with its nonsensical status of claiming 'fact' just because we have imagined something. We need, more than anything else, to remove these backwards ideas from all of our systems of power. There needs to be no political influence for imaginary ideas, however deeply culturally ingrained, and as we shift toward rational ideas of morality this should happen without most people blinking an eye. In the same way as we delete prejudice from our laws, we don't then allow it (or rather shouldn't allow it) to have a say in what we do. So when we delete the structurally similar to prejudice 'faith' from our laws, by ridding ourselves of silly laws like those against blasphemy, we also need to remove its place in creating influence. For all of the reasons that I claimed we need to begin looking seriously at atheism in chapter 5, we need to begin seriously examining our desire to have people of religious influence involved in any form of politics.

THE CATASTROPHIC TACTICAL FAILURE OF LEFTISM

It is no surprise that rational morality will tend toward the left in areas of politics. Leftists tend to value people over money, generally campaigning more for things like freedoms, equality, help for the less fortunate and nonhuman interests. Similarly those on the right tend to represent our selfish and

---

[95] http://www.bbc.co.uk/news/uk-17021831

irrational side, campaigning for ideas like tax breaks, tougher immigration laws and helping those who financially succeed to do so even further. Of course parties on both sides have tried to centralise over the years, in a bid to increase popularity, but these are generally identified characteristics. It is perhaps an unwritten rule in neutral discussion not to note the left as altruistic and rational, and the right as selfish and system-orientated; an unwritten rule perhaps upheld by the right wing insistence that they have some magical knowledge of economics holding up their otherwise irrational decisions. This magical knowledge thereby meaning we should be grateful for their selfishness. I don't follow this bizarre rule and I believe we need to cast it out like other prejudices. This bizarre relativist idea that every opinion is equally true is utter nonsense and doesn't sit well with what we know about the world. *Right wing* politics is, in ideology at least, the most irrational type that there is.

However, the left has seemingly begun isolating themselves more than creating a viable alternative to the irrational, selfish world we live in. I do not hold the life experience of being involved with many leftist organisations, which is why I make the comments that I do on how the left doesn't (or at least no-longer does) appeal to many people, especially those like me.

Isolating Language Use

The one movement I have previously taken part in, purely because I was motivated by the vast numbers of victims in comparison to other irrational prejudices, is the nonhuman animal rights movement. For a while, at least, I immersed myself in it, and you can perhaps see (in previous chapters where I've referenced it) my disappointment with the way the movement has gotten lost. Perhaps it was never 'found' in the first place by many participants. However, one insight my involvement gave me concerns the use of language.

Many in the rights movement for nonhumans spot that emotion is a useful tool in advocacy, and so begin tirades based on showing their feelings to others as a way of advocating their cause. As a result, we see groups placing huge emphasis on words like 'compassion', 'cruelty' and 'love'. Maybe I speak as a confused ex-farmer's son, but these words don't strike me as the type that will connect with real people. They might get other sensitive, emotive people on board, but I don't hang around in these sorts of groups (does anyone?). I don't really know anyone who values the idea of 'love' such that it will motivate them to act in some specific way without other factors. Similarly, I think the same of 'compassion': a term I only hear used by non-animal rights people when scratching for a way to distance themselves from an act which they morally disagree with.[96] Even emotive people, who might be easily influenced by such words, would surely be easily influenced also by the pressures of others who disagree with the subjective nature of them. That's how society works in enrolling the norms into most of its members, through social pressure. And hence these kinds of subjective, emotive words cannot be of that much use when aiming primarily at a small, easily affected group.

The reason why these words are so ineffective is that they are entirely based in subjective, or worse, spiritual foundations. They don't provide an outright reason to be abhorred by events, or to be supportive of solutions, but rather reach out to people's irrational side. They implore us to 'just act, don't think about it, just act'. And with all due respect, that's the last thing someone who wants to foster concern and change should be doing. We need people to think critically, evaluate the problems and start contributing to change. Acting out of subjective, personal instincts is how we get into a mess, not how we climb out. If one falls into a large hole by leaping forwards and flailing their arms with their eyes closed, one isn't often going to get out by doing the same thing. We cannot, in essence, fight ignorance with better intentioned ignorance.

---

[96] It is perhaps not surprising that people grasp at words like this. As I have explained throughout, the moral landscape at current is a confused and at best apathetic one. When people feel morally abhorred, it is not a shock that they scratch for subjective words like 'compassion' to describe how someone should be acting.

Communities

It is understood in leftist circles that the key to survival, and progression, is to create communities. Give people who care about leftist politics a place they can go where others care about it, a way by which they don't have to submit to the problematic norms currently perpetuated in society. Indeed youth subcultures like this are, historically speaking, the place where revolutions themselves are pollinated.

However, it seems to me that the aspect of community has over grown its usefulness. Look in circles of vegans and you see an overwhelming, bizarre nature of characters, mainly hostile to non-vegans, or else incredibly loving and sensitive 'hippy' types. Similarly, look to anarchists or socialists and you see the same hostility or sensitivity, just with a different focus. In both is also a sense of inward looking; we like to socialise with others like us, and sub-cultures like this are no different. Even the use of language (it's all 'patriarchal masters' 'compassionate living' and 'pigs' instead of 'police') is incredibly inward looking, and is enough to put off all but the most committed in those groups from getting further entrenched in the group norms. More time appears to be spent inwardly examining complex issues of hierarchy and the language we should use to describe it, than is spent being normal people and getting other normal people involved. A focus on purity rather than what's right.

As a rational matter, this is a problem. I don't come from a background of any sort of ethical alliance, and indeed would never have come to one were it not the result of my rationalist tendencies and happening across the right chain of events. Reaching normal people involves participating in society and approaching issues in ways which are not going to provide isolation, but rather appeal objectively to everyone's rational capabilities. Attack irrational beliefs, promote the rational.

Similarly (and this is especially true of the burgeoning vegan movement), people coming to veganism through rationality might be well placed not getting involved with the current communities at all. As we have already discussed, current vegans are not good markers of rationalism at all, and in marking my rational views to other vegans I have received a great number of spiritual, almost judgemental responses. Those vegans who see the problems with welfare regulation campaigns (abolitionists) tend to be more open to rational thinking. However, even then, the abolitionist movement itself was founded by Francione: an academic who values spirituality to such a degree that his own advocacy involves 'principles of non-violence', 'compassion' and 'ahimsa' rather than any meaningful, objective, rational terms. Such findings led me to see there were actually no foundations for rational veganism in current literature and other than a growing number of advocates who are coming to veganism through rationality, we are not likely to find much rationality in existing groups[97]. As such, people seeing the rational value of veganism might be best to start building new support communities themselves, with help from the current branch of rationalist vegans–leftist ideas like veganism might need *rational* communities, but they do not need spiritual gurus. And these communities, moreover, need to be open to new people and societal acceptance in order to grow. Joining current communities in hope of changing their minds might be as useful as joining Christian communities armed with atheist arguments. As Thomas Pain put it, "To argue with a person who has denounced reason…is like administering medicine to the dead".[98]

Rational Groups

Perhaps the biggest pragmatic advantage of a theory like rational morality is that it encompasses so many goals, all with a simple understanding and clear method. Like how the

---

[97] There are, to my knowledge, two places where rationalists can expect to find good support for becoming vegan online, and both groups appear on the social networking site facebook. They are Vegan:UK (http://www.facebook.com/groups/veganuk/) and Vegans for Reason and Science (http://www.facebook.com/vegansforreasonandscience).
[98] Quote taken from the series of articles written by Thomas Paine entitled 'The Crisis'. This one is in the March 21st, 1778 letter.

umbrella of physics ties together physicists of great variation, under shared goals to understand the world, so does rational morality; seeking, as it does, to put forth a scientific model of morality that isn't based on the personal ideas of its participants, but rather proof and evidence. Like with any science, disagreements will happen, but evidence will be the preserve of truth.

This is a very important practical step. All science benefits from the acceptance of needs for evidence and reason, as it stops great divides in opinion being either ever-lasting or disastrous for the subject as a whole. This is something that the current moral movements are in dire need of. They are based around personal intentions and with such little evidence or reason that it is hard to see that shared goals exist. As a result different people take up different tactics and the movement is divided and rendered useless due to a society confused about the subject, which in turn is formed through a muddled approach by the movement in question and inconsistent views about the movement being put across to society.

There is no better example of this than the nonhuman rights movement; which, as so often, is also the easiest for me to comment on. I wrote an article for a magazine I co-edit in which I described the different factions within the animal rights movement, and from which four distinct groups could be named. There are Conservationists, who don't believe in animal rights per se but often use the language of rights to push the interests of endangered mega fauna or other big species. There are Welfarists, who also don't believe in animal rights per se, admitting that the only concern is how we treat animals, not that we exploit them at all. This group also often use animal rights language and methods, but do so to better conditions or dissolve individual cruel farming practices. There are New Welfarists, who use tactics like Welfarist campaigns and single issue campaigns (like Conservationists use, aiming at abolishing certain uses), but actually believe that animals have a right not to be exploited at all. And finally, there are Abolitionists, who act in tandem with their beliefs that animals have a right not to be exploited, and they promote veganism and conduct abolitionist advocacy or vegan education. The latter group is honest about their intentions; the previous three use whatever will help their individual campaigns at the moment, thereby helping to cultivate this confused culture of what animal rights actually means. Arguably this does great harm in the mid and long term for the sake of short term public attention or donations.

These are four distinct and increasingly feuding positions. However, as mentioned throughout the sections on animals, there is vast evidence that shows Welfarism doesn't work. This is backed by legal and economic theory, and shown to be correct by real world events and figures in my opinion. There is also vast evidence to show that Conservationism, of the most popular type which indulges animal rights language, is completely irrational. They mainly focus on saving species from extinction rather than bothering about the interests of sentient individuals. These black and white pieces of reasoning show three of the four mentioned positions to be of no use, or at least of extremely limited use, and yet the remaining position, abolitionism, is easily the least populated of them and is the one most often attacked for its insistence on speaking about the aforementioned evidence. At best, advocates in these causes appear confused. A theory of morality as both rational and evidence-based provides compelling reason to stop all of this nonsense and focus on being honest, rational and scientific; focusing on improvement and progression rather than personal conjecture. Differences in opinion need only exist when no honest evidence does. Most groups of moral concern, as a result, would be united.

'Being' an advocate

This same analysis of animal rights shows something else rather important. The willingness of the factions to argue, without use of evidence, or without valuing of it, does show a remarkable moral confusion. More than anything, it shows that the advocates themselves are not involved with these movements as a matter of moral obligation, which they clearly think is a matter of personal taste (unless they simply misunderstand what truth is, or means). Rather, many are advocates as a social matter. They play the *role* of advocate, which involves doing what advocates do and acting how advocates act. Get a mohawk or dreadlocks, wear advocacy t-shirts, do the campaigns that other advocates do, be 'for' that issue when speaking with your friends, share campaigns in social media status updates, etc. These are supposedly tactical ideas, and yet it may well be the case that people fulfil them not primarily because they believe them effective, but rather as they think this is how advocates act. And they like to *be* advocates.

This is compelling, as I discussed earlier that no one's brain works in an irrational manner. Everyone makes the decisions they think are most supported. So when welfarist or conservationist advocates, for instance, are shown evidence that their own position is flawed, if they do not then change their position this shows either that they do not understand the value evidence has (and so believe faith to be a fine way of backing up ideas), or that they have ulterior motives for being advocates other than doing what's right (which is an intention that slips down to second on the list of importance). Such motives probably include fulfilling the social role of 'advocate' rather than having genuine empathy for the cause. Whilst we can approximate that many simply do not know the evidence or logic that counters the position which they hold, it seems illegitimate to say that this is the case for all advocates. To label it sympathetically, though, there must be some.

So there also must be a motive, and if not one of these two options (wanting to be an advocate, or wanting to do what's right) then undoubtedly it is profit based: investment in resources or groups built around these flawed ideas, or jobs dependant on continuing to fulfil the role. Most likely individual persons will not have these great financial investments, but will either not understand the role of reason in truth (understandable given the inability of 'animal rights' people to put this importance across in general) or be 'playing advocate' as a social matter, and thus have much to lose in identity by coming out of the closet, so to speak, against the ideas they have built into their very selves. Perhaps, as I hypothesise is the case with many New Welfarist advocates I have spoken to, it is a case of not wanting to admit that the past 20 years of their lives have not been utilised in the successful way which they thought their social status as 'an advocate' had guaranteed.

Science largely solves the problem of factionalism (including the problem of social status), by making sure that everyone working on the subject, or advocating any position, is aware of the need for evidence. Truth is the name of the game, not 'being' a scientist, and so this reliance on evidence is even built into the identity of scientists. As a result, there are relatively few times in which people within science hold to positions that are demonstrably untrue.[99] Similarly, those who stick to those propositions which are demonstrated as false tend to be cast away from their scientific reputation and forced into the world of non-academia. Only an area like quantum mechanics, where there is often doubt as to the correct answer, allows for factions of any degree, and even here nonsensical factions (like the three counter-productive factions in the nonhuman rights movement) are not tolerated under the academic umbrella.

If we could do the same in morality as with science, by teaching it as a rational subject, making sure advocates are aware that evidence is what matters and creating a culture where those with no respect for truth or evidence are cast into ignored roles, then the benefit would be massive. I've shown that morality can become a science, and reason appears to show that it would benefit greatly from becoming one. Surely science itself would also benefit, as people in general came to trust reason rather than requiring their own personal and spiritual beliefs.

---

[99] It still happens undoubtedly, but is much rarer.

9. A Sensible Conclusion – Rational Discourse

RATIONAL DISCOURSE

Within the theory of morality as a rationalist concept, there are 'moral facts' which need to be defined. Moral facts are purely provable by relation to evidence. Morality becomes a product of rationality, and if we were to choose to adopt a core principle (like we do with other sciences) that 'we ought to be rational', then we would be pushing the formulated theory of morality into scientific terms. This is purely factual and needs no assumptions beyond that which we need to investigate other methods of truth. Indeed, as I have attempted to show, it is not even a meaningful charge to doubt that we should be rational. The obligation to be rational is a necessary one so long as truth is what we are digging for, and if truth isn't what we are digging for then why bother with theories, ideas or action at all? We would all just be whatever we think we are, science and morality wouldn't exist, whilst you and I would be equally obliged to kill each other and ignore each other; with neither having a truth value on any scale whatsoever. The 'ought to be rational' is the most rational 'ought' that could exist, and so forms the most compelling theory of morality even in the face of the most initially compelling scepticism.

Many posit the marker of truth to be in the constraints of free speech, and they would be right. If we do not listen to ideas and interact with them (even with explicit nonsense, with which we can interact only so far as to show it is indeed nonsense) then we've no hope of finding truth, so everyone should be allowed a right to put their opinions across on some level. However truth doesn't just come from open, free speech, but also from rational speech. In discussions of science, for example, all views are not given equal footing: if someone has no evidence to back up their pseudo-scientific beliefs, but they want to argue them anyway and do so against the tide of scientific evidence, they tend to be ignored. And rightly so–this is how rational discourse works. We'd get nowhere if we ignored theories that have evidence, in favour of ideas that have none. So the scale of attention is a sliding one starting with rationally supported ideas at the top, and only relying on investigating irrational ideas if the most sensible ones fail.

Rational discourse is the thing that keeps important subjects on track, progresses with the reason of what we already know and draws conclusions upon the arrival of new evidence or the appearance of new rational points. It stops repetition of evidently false assumptions and claims, and halts the hijacking of intelligent progression by those who wish their opinions to be mounted as fact without having undergone the necessary checks. It stops made up gibberish being considered fact and prejudice from being considered valid government policy (or at least it should be allowed into discussion so it can do so).

Rational discourse, in this respect, is entirely missing from moral conversations. As discussed in the previous chapter, advocates of moral causes tend to stick rigidly with positions against the tide of reason and this is neither rational nor objectively honest. Hence rational discourse is the first thing that has to change. Advocates do not need training in scientific belief in order to adopt rational morality they simply need a rational change of opinion.

POST-MODERNISM: FAITH WITHIN ACADEMIA

In academia, this ignorance of rationality is often known as post-modernism. Post-modernism attacks science for a variety of reasons; post-modern feminists, for example, believe that rationality is the preserve of patriarchal norms which oppress women. This is no truer than saying the commissioning of new buildings was once used as a practice to involve slaves, and thus oppress non-whites, so buildings are racist. Logic is completely missing from these arguments and it is clear that causation is being implied where there is no direct relation. Yes, rationality is typically known as a male trait—just as in certain centuries the building of houses might have been the work of slaves—but this doesn't mean that the oppression is sourced from the one factor being mentioned. It wasn't rationality or logic that allowed men of previous eras, and many men still today, to oppress women, any more than it was buildings that oppressed black slaves. It was, in fact, completely the opposite: sexist and racist attitudes are the preserve of anti-rational thinking, and it was these that caused the oppression. As I've explained throughout, prejudice is as irrational a viewpoint as one can get.

As such, it is difficult to see why there is any need to engage with these arguments further than pointing out that one vital flaw. We need to accept that racism and sexism are still issues today, even in the traditionally white male-ruled Western world where we have seen female heads of state (Germany, the UK) and black heads of state (USA). Rape is still a problem, women still get less average pay for the same jobs and non-whites are still over-represented in prison populations. It takes an irrational view of the world to ignore these kinds of issues. But to posit that the cause of this sexism or racism is in some way just the advocacy of rational, consistent thinking is just absurd.

I don't think I am being unkind, as these theories which start with such poorly formed assumptions about the world do not deserve time be spent looking at their results, unless there are extraordinary circumstances. The fact that any academic can get away with making post-modernist arguments like this whilst keeping their job is a call for all of academia to be more scientific and more valuing of evidence. However, if you believe I have been unkind in not indulging these ideas, there are plenty of people who have spent their time providing in-depth analysis of their ideas (which, truthfully, shouldn't even be needed as a basic analysis shows the flaws). A good start would be Paul R. Gross and Norman

Levitt's all-encompassing 1994 book 'Higher Superstition: The Academic Left and its Quarrels with Science'.

The only further thing we need to note, as far as I am concerned, is that post-modernism is a form of faith-based thinking. This will already be obvious to some as it ignores evidence, posits entire subjects of studies based upon testable and incorrect assumptions about the world, and maintains that it does not even have to listen to rational arguments on the basis that they are somehow causing problems by their nature. The only way it differs from religious views of the world is that the authority it refers to is other post-modernist thinkers rather than a deity. Faith is the over-arching problem–not just in society, but in academia, in politics, in everything.

FAITH MUST GO

I've argued that a society that respects faith does more than just harbour religious intentions and belief. Far from it, if we deem faith a sufficient way of forming opinions, then everyone will be scarred by this mistake. It is faith that underpins all instances of people choosing not to listen, choosing not to act, or choosing not to change their minds when shown. Faith can be dangerous, or it can be harmless, and rationally speaking it will probably manifest in any society as both (ie, people taking comfort in fairy tales, but also an extremist section who enact violently upon delusions we have helped them to justify). Religious belief has a very specific irrational method. It consists of 'personal' truths, explicitly, and asks people to accept them. Secular faith, or prejudice, is different in that it holds explicit the idea that we don't need to be consistent to be right or to be respected. And if we look hard enough, I bet we can find secular faith to be present in most (if not all) well known rationalists, and this is shown especially well by the long standing belief many have in classic moral realism. It's shown even better by the liberal rationalists who seem oddly distracted when it comes to nonhuman animals. Faith doesn't just exist in religion; it's upheld in all manner of bad arguments and inconsistent positions within society.

One cannot overestimate how important the end of faith is. We don't need to wage war on people of faith, or outwardly attack people with religious beliefs. That would be unnecessarily hostile and immoral. We need to wage war on societal faith itself, respecting people whilst opposing faith at all times, and always considering reason and consistency the pinnacle of what we need to attain. We don't need, for instance, to *personally* attack religious points of view. However, if we need to defend why they are not being considered as panellists for a serious debate, we shouldn't be shy about defending reason by pointing to exactly why such irrational ideas have no place in civilised debate. There is a difference between rational arguments and hostile aggression, and rationalists tend to toe this line very well (not that their opponents are open to admitting this). I wholeheartedly support this method.

The threat in removing faith from society, so they say, is of losing morality. Many people claim we need religion to be moral, as there is no rational basis for being nice to each other. As I have argued at length, this simply isn't the case; if morality is rationally useful then it will fit into science and not need holding up by a plethora of folk tales, bad philosophy and pseudo-science. It will be governed by rationality and evidence like other pragmatically useful sciences such as physics or chemistry. A wonderful little book entitled 'Why We Believe in God(s). A Concise Guide to the Science of Faith' by J. Anderson Thomson, with Clare Aukofer, is a great resource on the matter of religion not being the corner stone of morality. It explains, from most perspectives one can imagine, in concise but thorough detail, exactly how and why humans are prone to faith. It explains it all right back to the beginnings of our evolutionary history and is backed up in hard, rational science every step of the way.

The most telling part is in its discussion on why the claim that we need religion to be moral is false. To do this, Thomson explains the scientific discovery of Mirror Neurons: the process by which the same neurons fire when I raise my left arm as when I see someone else raise their left arm. 'These neurons "mirror" the behavior of the other, as if the observer were performing the same action'. Thomson goes on to explain, in wonderfully persuasive, scientific rhetoric, that science is catching up with what we already observe and explaining morality rationally:

'Fundraisers understand this [mirror neurons] at some level. They can recite all the statistics about child hunger in the world without much effect on the typical person, but if they show that person a picture of one starving child, he or she will be much more likely to donate...We could feel the pain of loss and hopelessness, and our heartstrings would not allow us to sit by and do nothing.

We often hear that if it weren't for religion, we would be immoral and unethical. Mirror neurons resoundingly refute this. We literally feel others' pain, and that induces in us empathy, distress, and the urge to help. Our brains are ethical by design.'

This backs up rational morality, as I have been explaining it, with the kind of wonderful evidence that science is always capable of uncovering. Empathy is a rationally made instinct that is very useful for us to have. It is as useful for finding truth as is an intelligent, inquisitive mind. Following on, morality is a rational construct, in the exact same way as physics is, and both should be covered under the umbrella of truth finding that science refers to. They may not deal with the same types of facts, but undoubtedly they overlap constantly and should inform one another like any two types of science. Morality shouldn't posit claims that are physically impossible and physics shouldn't undertake research which is morally impossible.

EMOTION *CAN* BE RATIONAL

One other thing that Thomson's analysis teaches us is that emotion is rational. As earlier stated, the media depiction of rationality as some cold, unforgiving state of mind is nonsense. It is as rational (and as psychologically natural) to react to disgusting acts with disgust, and heart wrenching acts with sorrow, as it is to react to physical stimuli with movement or a will to understand the stimuli. The media has no basis for making out rationality as emotionless; at least no basis above the profit it brings them for exploiting such cultural myths.

What is true about emotion, though, is that facts themselves don't live in it. Emotions might be rational reactions, however this doesn't mean they can't be mistaken–after all, as I have also argued throughout, independent moral facts that our intuitions are somehow struggling to find do not exist. Emotions, therefore, are not the marker for what is wrong and what is right. Once we know what is wrong and what is right, we can in fact train our intuitions and emotions to respond accordingly. Luckily enough, it may be the case that most things we are disgusted by (murder, rape, etc.) we should continue to be disgusted by as a rational matter. But it will also mean that we need to change our ideas on other aspects of life which we are perfectly happy with at current (eating animal products, voting for classical right wing politics, etc.) and others may need to amend their reactions to that which they see as naturally disgusting (i.e., some straight people might feel 'naturally' disgusted by some 'unknown to them' concept of homosexuality, but this doesn't make homosexuality wrong, so much as their own intuitions deluded). Rational morality has to maintain an air of objectivity, and this might sit with or against our emotions, and with or against our intuitions. It doesn't mean emotion itself is always wrong or useless, though.

This objectivity is very simple and takes the scientific method of not fudging results. We can't amend what is rationally moral or immoral by reference to our own personal opinions. It might very well be the case that it is rational to allow people a freedom of speech that allows them to voice concern and disagreement with moral rules (indeed this is the scientific equivalent of being open to new theories, and should be maintained), but this doesn't mean that there isn't a basic moral obligation on those people protesting to halt it should they be shown evidence that they are wrong. We should be quick to listen to new ideas, but that should swiftly be followed by a critical analysis and willingness to interact with them, providing the evidence that we believe shows they are wrong, or else finding and accepting the evidence proving our own ideas wrong.

10. *The Changing Face of Ethics*

WHAT WE ARE

It is easy to look back over the ages and plot the remarkable moral development of humans. From an evolutionary point that saw us develop from lower primates with limited intellect, we have created societies that strive to value equality and fairness: achieving great technological steps and feats of science, alongside a more than equally great moral journey that has included the abolition of slavery based on race, sex and age, the protection of the young or the vulnerable, and the outlawing of many violent and societally disruptive acts. This is an impressive list for a bunch of apes!

Of course we can trace the moral characteristics of societies of ants, or vampire bats, but the ability to be able to survive without helping others, whilst still making the choice to do so is what truly what sets human beings apart. We see rare instances in nature of altruism, but nothing like in the examples we can pool from the human species. Were a technologically and intellectually advanced alien race to happen upon the earth tomorrow, it is surely this moral ability that they will note sets us apart from other animals on Earth.

This is not to denigrate our scientific achievements, quite on the contrary. Powered by stuff we dug up from the ground, and consisting of nothing but things we found lying around, we have managed to create rockets capable of flying us into space and landing on that tiny pale dot in the night sky. More impressively, we can now reach the almost invisible red dot even further away and send a robot to suss it out for us. And this is just in one tiny area of science. We've also created vaccines capable of halting intelligent viruses, cobbled together machines which can in hours compute equations that it might otherwise take a brilliant mathematician his whole career to do, build towering skyscrapers sturdy and clever enough to withstand earthquakes which we've never even experienced (just in case), and write theories and systems clever enough to work out the weather before it even happens. These are things to be genuinely proud and in awe of.

And yet my human pride in these achievements is nothing compared to the pride of being a member of the same species of the great heroes from history who showed that humans could do something even greater: sacrifice genetic desires in favour of doing what's right. People like Emily Davison, who so passionately believed in women's rights that she threw herself under the king's horse at Epsom Derby in protest, fully aware of the fatal injuries she might, and indeed did, receive. Or Frederick Douglass, a former slave who escaped and spent his life (and not to mention his wonderful oratory and literary ability) supporting the cause of abolition. Or how about Charles Darwin who—unwittingly, perhaps—fought everything he was in order to provide the truthful basis of the ideas which have freed us all from the emancipation of religion. As humans we are built to create leaps in technology, as it is that which provides us greater comfort or greater ability to reproduce safely. And yet the leaps we want in moral terms are an awful lot more dangerous, and an awful lot less safe. It is this courage to close our eyes and leap based on rational, moral ideas which truly sets us apart as a remarkable species.

WHAT ARE WE NOW?

Perhaps it is because we look with such admiration at the likes of Davison or Douglass that we now feel rather powerless about developing ethics any further. Perhaps we look at the great leaps we have made and think 'We've already gotten there'. Or perhaps, as I stated at the very start, we tend to believe that without a religious viewpoint there is no black and white moral causes any more.

This book was written with the aim of deleting that last theory; without God, morality is still alive and well.

Moreover, without God morality is *better* because it can be consistent and not arbitrarily decided based on mythical rules. And yet the former two theses are also false: we have a lot to be proud of in terms of morality, but we are certainly *not* there yet. In Davison's culture and in Douglass's culture there were times when the majority of people believed that these kinds of social changes were actually 'extreme' or pointless because 'we had already gotten there' when it comes to perfecting ethics. No society thinks it is currently morally wrong, or going to develop any further, instead *every* society sees itself as the pinnacle of morality. We are no different, and we are no less wrong.

A DIFFERENT KIND OF ETHICS, FOR A DIFFERENT KIND OF WORLD

It is this realisation—that we are no different from other societies in thinking we are morally perfect—that no doubt spurred an eventual change in moral code throughout the ages. But it is clear that for us to progress we must make one further realisation in our modern, economically organised society: heroic acts are no longer necessarily the result of direct action or bravery in the face of aggression. Undoubtedly it is these kinds of revolutions around the world that grab the headlines, and yet the real effective development and progression primarily comes in the form of personal responsibility and courage of a different kind.

We live in societies, for instance, where paying taxes is a moral obligation on behalf of those who have money (to help provide social services such as the NHS and the education system), and yet tax avoidance isn't technically illegal (plenty of loopholes exist, if you want to find them). We also live in societies where the largest amount of violence isn't on the streets and being aimed at strangers or enemies, but hidden away in family homes and supported by the sexual objectification of women, or else perpetrated against members of other species to satisfy our dining norms. In essence our greatest moral obligations are no longer necessarily in formal protest or direct action, but take the forms of choosing not to exploit the tax system, or choosing not to support sexist ideas about women's roles or choosing not to buy the products of immense suffering by the individuals of other species.

This might seem simple and easy compared to the struggles of Davison and Douglass, but moral problems still require a certain bravery to push them forwards; a bravery we should revere and be proud to stand up for. It is not easy, for example, to be a young male and to choose not to bow to peer pressure in objectifying women in magazines. It is not easy to be an educated business person (judged upon their ability to maximise profits) and not to seek the avoidance of tax. It is not easy to be a functioning member of a society that routinely provides the products of animal exploitation, whilst refusing to eat and wear what everyone else does. These examples do not require the bravery of a slave fleeing a plantation and opposing his oppressors, or a female facing death to further the rights of other women, but they still require a bravery for which you will likely never be applauded; a bravery to do what's right, without promise of recognition. Perhaps even a bravery not just to do what's right, but to talk to others about doing it also.

Yet this is what ethics in the modern world looks like. Remember the guy who chucked himself in the river at the Oxford-Cambridge boat race in 2012, to protest elitism? No? Or you do, but don't see him in the quite same light as Emily Davison? Well that's exactly my point. Even if the swimmer in question had a perfectly valid argument and protest, we now have a media with norms so wide-reaching that it is tailor made to neutralise any such perceived aggressive counter-action against societal views. People want to be comfortable, and media helps us to normalise with one another. Direct action is incredibly easy to outcast, and incredibly difficult to turn back once already outcast. A change in ethics in this era will come from intelligent, respectful exchanges and responsible, honest choices, else it won't come at all. Evidence can be found by looking at a surviving, all encroaching system of animal agriculture, in contrast to the continually jailed and pariah-labelled masked-intruders who broke in to rescue animals.

This is also where the weakness of mine, and every other moral theory in history, becomes relevant. No matter how well argued, or how well intentioned your ideas are, you can't make people act! And yet when this theory is published, and when it is looked upon in relation to other works of basic moral philosophy and science, I find there is cause for great optimism. This isn't a form of ethics like those I discussed in the first chapter; those theories which ask us to adhere to ideas which are, essentially, made up. This is a real, societally reflective theory of ethics, and it's one which we can all understand the reasons for and honestly hold to be true. That is monumentally important, at least in my opinion.

Why? Because if history teaches us anything about ethics, it's that only when the majority understand a moral movement will it become accepted. A moral theory which cannot be understood, or related back to reality (instead relying on powerful intuitions, or authority figures) can also therefore not hope to be successful in changing the state of things for the long haul. One might get short term obedience, but it just won't stick. The fact that rational morality is a scientific way of judging and understanding morality gives great reason to believe that it can be practically successful where no other theory could.

About The Author

Robert Johnson is a practical ethicist and philosopher of science, graduated in Philosophy from the University of Aberdeen. He specialises in the intersection of morality and rationality, whilst being a staunch advocate of science and evidence based endeavours.

His other interests and work lie primarily in animal ethics, where he has written numerous articles on animal welfare, animal rights and the irrationality within both, whilst standing up for non-human interests from a rational perspective. He currently resides in Aberdeen with his partner and their adopted cat, Riley.

Learn more at www.robertjohnson.org.uk

Printed in Great Britain
by Amazon.co.uk, Ltd.,
Marston Gate.